THE SOBO COOKBOOK

Lisa Ahier
with Andrew Morrison

photography by
Jeremy Koreski

THE SOBO

COOKBOOK

*Recipes from the Tofino Restaurant
at the End of the Canadian Road*

appetite
by RANDOM HOUSE

Appetite by Random House® and colophon are registered trademarks of Random House of Canada Limited

Library and Archives of Canada Cataloguing in Publication is available upon request

ISBN: 978-0-449-01585-8
eBook ISBN: 978-0-449-01586-5

Book design: Five Seventeen
Printed and bound in China

Published in Canada by Appetite by Random House®,
a division of Random House of Canada Limited,
a Penguin Random House Company

www.randomhouse.ca

10   9   8   7   6   5   4   3   2   1

I would like to dedicate this book to my husband, Artie, who has put his own dreams on the shelf to help me realize mine. I would like to publicly thank him for the sacrifices he made for me to go to the Culinary Institute of America; for taking a risk on a food truck long before they were fashionable; for being Mr. Mom when my workload is insane; and for letting me take credit that clearly belongs to us both. Thank you for never giving up.

Contents

Foreword
by Sarah McLachlan

Tofino is a truly magical part of the world, blessed with ancient conifers, miles of rugged coastline and a rich, vibrant culture of First Nations, artists, fishermen and loggers, and folks generally looking to live a cleaner, simpler life away from the rat race of the big city. It is also home to SoBo, one of my very favorite restaurants.

I was first lured to Tofino in 1989 by my best friend, who invited me to camp at her parents' cabin on Chesterman Beach. I instantly fell in love with the area's wild, infectious beauty; just being there felt like a whole different kind of alive. I have returned every chance I've got over the years, always yearning for the sense of belonging and calm I feel in the vastness of all that space and intense beauty.

Around the same time as my first daughter was born, so was the first incarnation of SoBo, based out of a soon-to-be-famous purple catering truck. Our local friends raved about this cool truck serving up amazing and fresh comfort food. It was an instant hit with us wet and tired wannabe surfers, looking for a jolt of energy to feed our hungry, aching bodies. After a few years, SoBo outgrew their original space and moved the truck to the Botanical Gardens where they could expand to manage the growing crowds. I loved going at sunset, eating outside and marveling at the surrounding forests

and art installations. My daughter and her friends, no longer babies, would wind their way through the labyrinth carved out of gnarled branches and salal with wild abandon. No adults allowed! Over time SoBo outgrew the truck altogether, and a few years ago they found their new and current home as a restaurant right in the heart of town.

SoBo is owned by Lisa and Artie Ahier and it is their kindness and warm familiarity that defines the energy of SoBo. Lisa and Artie and all of their staff are always ready and welcome to embrace the community through their doors. On more than one occasion, I've burst into today's SoBo late in the day, asking for an entire key lime pie, tray included (which I promise to bring back, and always do), and Lisa will offer up some fresh rhubarb to take home along with it, when it's still growing in their garden and there's none left in town to buy. I feel privileged to be a part of that world.

As for the food . . . From the dreamy smoked salmon chowder to the fresh fish tacos laced with mango and blueberry salsa, SoBo always serves up the perfect combination of salty and sweet. Lisa's cooking is infused with love, fresh, healthy ingredients and a subtle but sophisticated magic. It is the ultimate in modern comfort food, as she is not afraid to embrace the richest ingredients from her Southern roots—like the coveted and lusted-after polenta fries, which are heaven from a deep-fryer (but, after reading the recipe, I can see they aren't quite as fattening as I'd imagined!). If you're feeling more health-conscious, dishes like SoBo ceviche are lovely and light, and so befitting a warm summer night. Then there's the peanut sauce . . . oh my. I could, and would, put that on *anything*!

I know this book will become a staple in my kitchen—a way to bring SoBo to me when I cannot get to Tofino and eat at the restaurant itself. But if you haven't been to SoBo yet, for heaven's sake get yourselves there as soon as you can!

Introduction
by Andrew Morrison

Today SoBo is an aesthetically unassuming family restaurant that seats about 75 people in an open-concept dining room. There is a piano and a carefully considered wine list, but it's nothing fancy. It's about as far removed from pretension as the rugged town of Tofino it serves. The strength behind it is the marriage of two exceptionally creative people, Artie and Lisa Ahier. Their kids, Barkley and Ella, are the same age as my own, and they can't get enough of each other. We grown-ups share an abiding passion for food, and over the years (and many late, wine-soaked nights) our two families have become very close. We stay with them whenever we make the trip to Tofino, and our house is theirs on the rare occasions that bring them to the big city of Vancouver.

We first met in 2005. I'd come over on holiday with my wife and our two young sons, taking our old camper van across the Georgia Strait on a ferry from West Vancouver to Departure Bay, then driving across the spine of Vancouver Island on the often breathtaking Highway 4. I was writing about restaurants for a living (after nearly 20 years of working in them), penning weekly reviews for a local paper and feature articles for magazines. It was part of my job to suss out the best food in the province, but on this particular journey I wasn't looking to be wowed by anything except sunsets and sand. I was there to cook hot dogs over beach fires and roast marshmallows on embers while watching the stars make a fool of city life.

Early on day two we walked up the dusty road from our campsite to the Botanical Gardens, where we found ourselves alone in a quiet wilderness. The morning mist had lifted to reveal an elven paradise of lush gardens, moody waterfront and looming rainforest. The gardens were dotted with driftwood sculptures and crisscrossed by a labyrinth of trails that led to little clearings, gazebos and the rusted-out shell of an early 1970s bay window VW bus that was slowly but surely being claimed by the forest.

It was coming up on lunchtime when we made our way out to the gravel parking lot, which had nearly filled with cars. A line-up had formed at an old food truck across from the garden entrance. We hadn't seen a single person on our walk. Nor had we noticed the truck on our way in. Yet here it was, virtually surrounded by people. This was many years before the street food trend exploded, so I assumed it would be a lowly dispensary of bad burgers and greasy onion rings, run in an unhealthy, slipshod fashion. But we were famished, the fuel of our camp breakfast having long run out. I joined the long line.

It wasn't until a new SUV arrived and unloaded a Gore-Tex–clad pair of city slickers that I began to suspect that everything wasn't as I assumed. They joined the growing line behind me and didn't even so much as glance at the garden's entrance. Neither did the Lycra-wearing cyclists who quickly dropped their bikes to beat a pride of surfer locals to the back of the line (the latter group having emerged from an old station wagon with marijuana smoke pouring from its open doors). And still others came: young families with little kids, longboarders out cruising the paved roadside bike paths, more cyclists, more families, more surfers. Clearly, something either ridiculous or very special was going on. Whatever it was, it smelled great!

Fifteen minutes later, while sitting at a nearby picnic table and not a little amazed at having a face full of the finest fish taco I'd ever tasted (local line-caught halibut crowned with mango salsa), it all clicked. *I knew where I was!* The year before, I'd counted myself among all the foodies and restaurant pros from across the country who'd read with great interest *enRoute* magazine's incongruous inclusion of a Tofino eatery in its annual report on "Canada's Best New Restaurants." The top 10 list was a big deal, and so widely read that its editor sent out a personal letter to every restaurant included to warn them of the impending onslaught of new customers ("My advice to you," it summarized, "is brace yourself."). That year, the number-one spot was Mark McEwan's

elegant Bymark in downtown Toronto, a trophy restaurant for well-heeled brokers and all manner of suits besides. And then, inexplicably, at #9 was "a purple catering truck where people come from afar to see chef Lisa Ahier turn local produce, and organic meat and seafood, into socially conscious sophisticated takeout fare." I turned around and looked again at the line-up and then back at the truck, which was indeed purple, vividly recalling the writer's words and how I'd smirked doubtfully when I'd first read them. At the time, I couldn't help but wonder how a restaurant on wheels without table service could convince anyone in their right mind that it deserved to be on such a list. Surely it couldn't be superior to the many other candidates

that operated on a completely different plane, complete with sommeliers, busboys, candlelight and proper washroom facilities! And yet it was, and I was busily eating the reason why.

But how, I wondered, did such good, simple, soul-warming food end up here, at the very edge of the world?

The SoBo Story

Since the beginning—since well before we started serving fish tacos out of our purple truck in a parking lot—my husband, Artie, and I knew exactly what we wanted. We wanted to serve incredible food at prices that our friends could afford. It wasn't a brand-new idea, but we knew we could go at it with love and passion and bring to life something that was all our own. We wanted to take the best movements in contemporary cuisine—slow food, organic farming, local sourcing and multiethnic influences—and make them accessible in a natural and egalitarian way. We set out to serve anti-fast food, with regional ingredients and a global influence. To use a word from Tofino's surf slang, we wanted to serve food that was, simply, *killer*.

SoBo's success was almost immediate when we opened in 2003—within a few weeks, the lunch rush was becoming an all-day rush—but the menu we started out with was the result of a decades-long evolution. Artie and I are now firmly rooted in this rainy coast of British Columbia in the beautiful beach town of Tofino, but we began our lives in entirely different places: he in New Brunswick, where his family owned and ran a Dixie Lee Fried Chicken; me in Texas, where my mother managed a succession of restaurants that gave me my earliest cooking influences, Southwestern and Tex-Mex.

We first met in Florida, where Artie was skippering a private yacht and I was tending bar and cooking at an Irish pub, of all things. As Artie tells it: "After knowing Lisa for two years, one day I came in from a Chesapeake trip, and Lisa was just getting off work. I asked her for a date two nights later, and we've been together ever since." A few months later, I joined Artie aboard the yacht, cooking in the galley for the owners and their friends. In the cramped quarters of a 70-foot boat, we laid the foundations of the partnership that would eventually bring SoBo into being.

The next act of our lives unfolded in central Texas, at a lodge in the Fossil Rim Wildlife Center, a 2,500-acre zoological center and rare animal preserve. Artie, a lifelong naturalist, led tours through the preserve's sprawling property. During our time there, he got himself a two-page spread in *National Geographic*—he's pictured behind the wheel of a stripped-down Jeep in a collared shirt and safari hat, looking out at an ostrich and a crowd of antelope, all nosing up to him as if he's one of their own.

After three years at Fossil Rim, we heard that my father's health was failing, and I left work to be with him. The day before he passed away, he had a heartfelt conversation with Artie. He'd always

regretted not being able to see me go to university, and after watching me grow as a self-taught cook, he felt that chef school would be the key to our success. He made Artie promise that he'd get me to cooking school. I thought it was too expensive, but Artie insisted we'd make it work, and somehow we did. So we packed up, went on a summer camping trip to the Maritime provinces and signed in at the Culinary Institute of America in New York. It took my understanding of cooking techniques to a whole different level, and the rigorous standards of the Culinary Institute have formed the basis of my cooking ever since. Looking back, it was absolutely the best training available—truly the education of a lifetime. I've never been one to do anything

half-heartedly, and I went on to graduate with honors in 1996.

There was another life-changing aspect to my time at the Institute. While I was studying there, I had the opportunity to extern under Melissa Kelly at the Old Chatham Sheepherding Company Inn in the farmlands of upstate New York. She's a chef who has had a huge influence on my culinary values. She is dedicated to technique, takes no shortcuts and has an almost fanatical devotion to cooking. I've always had a crazy work ethic, but even I couldn't touch Melissa—she'd work 100-plus hours a week. I've been more inspired by her than anyone.

New York was also where the idea of SoBo started to take shape, though it would be a few more years before we'd make it out west. Before I finished at the Culinary Institute, I was given a project to design a restaurant on paper, with menus, logos, wine lists and all. I set my concept at South Beach in Miami: a tapas bar that served fish tacos. I called it the Sophisticated Bohemian, and it became the model we'd eventually use for SoBo in a much greener and quieter place.

Leaving New York, we headed back to my home state after signing on at Cibolo Creek Ranch, a remote, ultra-luxurious property in the high desert where I served as executive chef while Artie worked as general manager. There were ulterior motives—Artie was in his hardcore birding phase and knew that the Big Bend area of Texas was incredible for birds. As you can probably tell by now, being in unique settings has always been important to us. We both want to work where we want to live—that's the only kind of life that makes sense to us. At the helm of a $17-million property, catering to guests like Mr. Mick Jagger, we slowly settled into our professional lives. It wasn't easy. As Artie says, "I was anything but a cowboy, and Lisa was anything but a cowgirl, and the next years held some of the hardest hours we've ever worked. But our time there solidified our careers for the rest of our lives." Artie instituted bird walks and hired an archaeologist to lead guests on trips through the Texas drylands, while I set to the task of producing thoughtful ranch food, that didn't default to the heavy red-meat focused menus ranches usually do. I revived the old organic gardens, sourced free-range game and worked with local food co-operatives. Our three years at the ranch earned us notable reviews in *Gourmet*, *The New York Times*, *Food & Wine* magazine and a long list of others—not to mention an accidental *Vogue*

spread of me cooking over an old iron stove for models clad in clothes from Gucci and Saks Fifth Avenue! There were great people at Cibolo Creek whom we will always love, but as Artie says, we've always moved on when things got silly.

Artie had always wanted to come back to Canada, and as our time in Texas drew to a close we heard the West Coast calling us. We interviewed at a lodge in Ucluelet and visited the Sooke Harbour House, but the most naturally enticing area was Tofino. We knew that our future was here at the edge of Clayoquot Sound's ancient forests. We loved the people, loved the community and we were sure that we'd found our place. We started out by helping to open two resorts, but we knew that unless our work was truly our own, we'd never be able to see our dreams come to life. And so, in 2003, Sophisticated Bohemian, or SoBo as it quickly became known, was born.

We opened SoBo in a gravel parking lot behind one of Tofino's original surf shops. "At that time, it was about surviving," Artie remembers. "We had a house and our six-month-old son, Barkley, so we started with a food truck because that's all we could afford." We worked nonstop to get the business going, but the truth is that we couldn't have got off the ground without the support of our families. My mom came for six months every year in those early days, helping out with the kids and keeping our guests entertained. She hasn't been back to the coast for a few years now, but our regulars still talk about her all the time.

The news about our food spread around town, and before long SoBo was one of the community's chosen spots to chill out and chow down before hitting the waves or heading back to work. It was

definitely the funkiest spot in town—the kind of place where no one was in much of a hurry to leave. Around the tables, you'd see everything from gritty old builders on their lunch break to German tourists on van vacations and clean-cut hipsters cruising in for miso oysters and tofu pockets to go. And there was always me and the crew rocking it in the back, the kids toddling around in the play area and Artie bustling around maintaining the flow out front. For visitors, SoBo had the free-spirited feel of the West Coast, and we kept it fun, even when we were slammed. On the back of our first T-shirts, we printed, "Quite possibly the second best experience you can have in a parking lot."

In 2005, two years after SoBo opened, we left our humble beginnings in the parking lot and found a new home at the Tofino Botanical Gardens. We still served lunches out of the truck, but dinners became a more elegant affair, moving into a space that opened onto a lovingly tended garden. Shortly after the move we welcomed baby Ella to our family. I'll never forget that beautiful day in June, four weeks before my 45th birthday. After working the lunch rush on the truck, Artie, Barkley, my mom and I loaded up the car and drove across the Island to the hospital, and the next morning we were holding a perfect baby girl. Later that week, Ella was installed in a semi-permanent spot in a car seat next to the cash register, where she slept away the first few months of her life. We were dead set on not having a nanny—we'd waited so long to have kids and wanted to raise them ourselves, so somehow we made it work. I became much more reliant on my kitchen team, and some of my closest and dearest friends came to my rescue—chef Rick Moore, James Pocock, Aaron Walsh, Katrina Peters and pastry chef Jen Scott, who's still with me today. Bobby Lax and Jen Boulton were always there to take Ella for a quick jaunt around the garden, too.

We loved almost every minute of our time in the Botanical Gardens, but although our popularity grew our space did not, so three years later were faced with yet another move. The Conradi building in downtown Tofino is where we've been since 2008. With the addition of a Wood Stone pizza oven, a full bakery and a home-meal line, things have changed. But nothing much has *really* changed. SoBo is still one of the most talked-about eateries on the West Coast, it's still as original and fresh as it was the day we opened, and it still strikes a balance between my culinary skill and Artie's vision and creativity.

So here we are, 10 years later, doing what we've always done—living in beautiful surroundings, serving incredible food, making our guests feel like our best friends and doing our best to shape our lives into a balanced work of art. Our values are based on openness, democracy, passion and commitment, and they extend to every level of our operation. We're all in it together at SoBo, which is a rare thing in this business. Settled into the salt air of the Clayoquot coast, we've managed to create a unique culinary culture in the midst of one of the world's most pristine and inspirational landscapes. SoBo is a product of our professional experiences, of course, but it is also a product of the soulful, stunningly beautiful place we'd found ourselves, between the thick forests and the wild sea.

Enjoy,
Lisa

Tofino

Tofino is a uniquely magnetic small town in British Columbia, a frontier outpost that has always attracted a different stripe of character. It sits on the wild west coast section of Vancouver Island known as Clayoquot Sound, just beyond the Pacific Rim National Park on the northern tip of the Esowista Peninsula. Its environs, colored by a palette of grays, greens and blues, are as pristine and entrancing as they are wild and rugged. To get there, you really have to want to.

The Nuu-chah-nulth and Tla-o-qui-aht First Nations had already been living in the area for many thousands of years when the first Europeans—fur traders, mostly—arrived in the late 18th century. The name Clayoquot derives from Tla-o-qui-aht, the name of the First Nation who lived there and were known as "strange or foreign people." By the 1850s, the Europeans' trading post was flourishing on nearby Stubbs Island, with the Tofino townsite slowly growing in its shadow across the water. Tofino was named after Spanish King Charles III's hydrographer Captain Vincente Tofiño de San Miguel, by two Spanish naval commanders, Dionisio Alcalá-Galiano and Cayetano Valdés, who sailed to Clayoquot Sound in 1792.

Though it eventually attracted a doctor (1906) and the Anglican Church (1913), Tofino remained a rough-and-tumble sort of place through the two world wars, and was nicknamed Tough City for its tempestuous weather and geographic isolation. From 1913 until 1952, every 10 days the S.S. *Maquinna* would deliver people, mail and supplies from Victoria. Finally, in 1959, a 130-kilometer (just over 80 miles) road was built across the mountains from Port Alberni to the ocean; an unpaved snake reserved exclusively for the booming logging industry (except on weekends).

The access challenges and rumors of rideable waves attracted new pioneers during the 1960s. A whole generation of cold-water surfers, draft dodgers, artists and representatives from every walk of hippiedom would come to call it home. Some lived in town, but many lived in the countless makeshift camps and squatter shacks that were sprouting up in the beach-hugging forests. These would later either be demolished to make room for the Pacific Rim National Park or replaced with million-dollar vacation homes, but by then the die had been effectively cast. No matter how many fancy resorts and retreats the future would bring, Tofino would always be a laid-back town marked by a rejection of convention and defined by a deep respect for the immediate environment. When the ancient cedar forests of Clayoquot Sound were

threatened with decimation by the timber industry in the early 1990s, the people stood their ground in collective protest. Their confrontation with logging companies and police made international headlines and culminated in the largest and most effective act of peaceful civil disobedience in Canadian history. Over 800 arrests were made, but the community's courage and selflessness resulted in the multitude of new protections included the 1995 Clayoquot Sound Land Use Decision.

Today, with the switch from a resource-based economy to one anchored by ecotourism, the area remains "different"; a fun-loving place with an average age of 34. Visitors in the summer months can swell the local population of 1,700 to over 25,000 on some days, with more than 750,000 visitors coming to the area every year. Most come for the sea kayaking, whale watching, bear watching, storm watching, hiking, birding, surfing and skateboarding, but some come for the food—obsessively good food made with fresh, local ingredients.

Residents of Tofino have incredibly high standards and like to know where their food comes from. Their passion is celebrated at the annual Oyster Festival, which has been "keeping Tofino's population growing since 1997" (yes, that is its official slogan), and at the Tofino Food & Wine Festival, held every year since 2003 in the lush Botanical Gardens. And for the entire month of May, nearly every restaurant and hotel in the town (and in the nearby village of Ucluelet) indulges in Feast, an earnest celebration of boat-to-table cuisine. The driving force behind all the events and festivals is the chefs and restaurateurs, the majority of whom banded together in 2010 to form the Tofino-Ucluelet Culinary Guild, working together to guarantee a reliable supply of local, seasonal and sustainable ingredients for its member kitchens, SoBo included.

The phrase "the end of the road" often has negative connotations, but in Tofino, just a stone's throw from where the Trans-Canada Highway officially comes to a complete stop, it's all good.

Food Philosophy

I feel very strongly about freshness and pure simplicity when it comes to food. Great recipes will only make great meals if you use great ingredients. Fortunately for SoBo, I'm passionate about finding great ingredients. I take pride in cooking with integrity and honesty, and in showcasing the flavors of foods in their natural state. As you'll see from the photos in this book—they were all shot in natural light without food stylists or artificial props—SoBo food isn't always picture-perfect on the plate. We put substance before style. No bells or whistles, just good food.

When I started cooking professionally 20 years ago, the expression "farm to table" wasn't commonly heard. Chez Panisse in Berkeley and European chefs had always been on board with buying food daily and preparing ultra-fresh product, but the notion of good, ethical sourcing wasn't talked about much in North America. Despite this, I learned early in my career that you have to start with the best, freshest and most interesting ingredients. I took that lesson seriously and it has always helped me create simple, seasonal and regionally distinct recipes. We don't purchase tomatoes in winter or strawberries for Valentine's Day, for example, so when these incredible gems start to show up in the summer we greet them with joy, knowing that we can use them to mark the new season with special dishes. These days, my menus are almost entirely inspired by product—I'll come across something incredible, like mussels from Quadra Island, and then find a way to use them that will show them at their best.

SoBo is about respecting people and the planet. We value the independent over the industrial, and we're always mindful about how we can reduce the burden that the food system places on our environment. From the day SoBo opened, we've made local and organic food the defining aspect of SoBo's culinary identity. Our local area is home to some incredible farmers, foragers and fisherfolk, and we work closely with dozens of them to make sure the best ingredients possible are coming to our door. Thinking local has always worked well for me, whether it was the homemade sheep cheeses I cooked with at the Old Chatham Sheepherding Company Inn in New York or the organic greens and fresh meats of Cibolo Creek in Texas. I'm always looking for food that's been produced with care, and I want to trust in and connect with my suppliers. After all, they're the ones with the intimate knowledge of the ingredients, the little idiosyncrasies you need to know about to bring the flavors out in powerful ways.

Getting to know our suppliers gives us confidence that our food is sourced in an ethical way. For our first three or four years, red meats weren't a part of our menu, as we had trouble finding products that we thought were ethical. Now we have numerous farms that are going back in time, letting their animals graze on grass instead of grains and giving them ample space to have a decent life, so we know that the meat and poultry we serve has been raised in humane conditions. Fish purchasing and sustainability is a subject that is debated endlessly in Tofino; personally, for the restaurant and for cooking at home, I do not purchase farmed fish. Generally, I stay with hook-and line-caught fish; prawns and shrimp from baited traps; and by catch and aquaculture for scallops, oysters, mussels and clams. I can say that because I have the luxury of living in an area where wild fish is fairly abundant and affordable, and because my trusted fisher suppliers can keep me informed on what is happening in our local waters. We don't belong to any particular organization, but Seachoice, Oceanwise and Streamkeepers all have good guidelines for smart ethical choices in your particular area. I would suggest you develop a relationship with your local fish and seafood market and don't be afraid to ask questions.

SoBo is also about passion. It's our real magic ingredient! As Artie says, "Very few restaurants seem to be done for passion, and for a restaurant to work it has to be driven by passion. There also has to be experience and expertise if you want to survive. I think the thing with SoBo is that we combine all three. We can't help but have passion for what we do: If the love for it wasn't there, we'd go do something else."

And that love is the essence of what we do and why we do it. Many of us are tired of the cynical, market-driven culture that surrounds us; we want to be involved with like-minded people, the ones who see the value in filling their lives with love and fun. My food philosophy is rooted in those values, and I know part of SoBo's appeal stems from the culture of love and connection we've created around us. Passion, connection and love. And good food. That's about it. That's SoBo.

Cook's Notes

This book is an open-hearted passing on of my knowledge and experience to you. I believe in food that has natural beauty and that makes you feel good not only while eating but also after eating. For me, the dream cookbook is something that's useful, so *The SoBo Cookbook* isn't supposed to be a showpiece. We've focused on recipes that are simple, fun and accessible. It's real food for real people.

Ingredients are really important to me, so I want to take some time to talk through some of the key ingredients you will see in the recipes in this book; to explain a little bit about them, and why I use them in my cooking. After all, a well-stocked pantry makes cooking, and life, easier!

Sauces, Syrups, Vinegars and Pastes

SOY SAUCE

There are many choices these days when it comes to soy sauce. Wheat-free, reduced-sodium, black, white and even mushroom soy sauce. I usually use light or white soy sauce as a condiment for my sushi and dark soy sauce, tamari (which contains proportionally less wheat than soy sauce) or mushroom soy sauce in sauces.

COCONUT MILK

Coconut milk is available in cans at most grocery stores these days and is excellent in soups, curries and vegan foods. Some brands are totally blended, others have the fat at the top and the milk below. I prefer the latter. I like to use the top fat layer for sautéing.

MAPLE SYRUP

Canada produces 80% of the world's maple syrup, with Quebec being the main source. I only use pure maple syrup in my cooking, whether it is lighter (Grade A) or darker (Grade B). Blended maple syrups often have unwanted corn syrup or cheaper sweeteners added, so stay away from those.

VINEGAR

Vinegar adds zingy acidic notes to foods, and it's also a time-tested preservative. Apple cider is my preference for pickling, balsamic for depth, white wine or champagne for more subtle recipes and red wine or sherry vinegar for salads. There are numerous varieties of fruit, wine and grain vinegars. Play around with them and expand your horizons.

RICE VINEGAR

A mild Asian vinegar made from fermented rice. I prefer the Japanese variety, which is essential to a few of my dressings and sushi rice. I haven't found a western substitute for rice vinegar.

MIRIN

This Japanese cooking wine adds sweetness to many Asian sauces. Equal parts sugar and water, with the sugar fully dissolved in the water, can work as a substitute. It's used in teriyaki sauce.

HOT SAUCE

Tabasco, Frank's RedHot and Louisiana are all brand names of a cayenne pepper sauce made from chilies and vinegar. Everyone I know has their favorite but Tabasco or Frank's RedHot XTRA Hot are certainly more intense so be careful if you're substituting brands in recipes. You'll see sambal oelek called for occasionally in the recipes; this is an Asian condiment made purely from chilies, with no added ingredients like vinegar or garlic, just pure chili flavor.

MUSTARD

From the elegant Dijon to the generic yellow or hot Chinese varieties, mustard is a key feature in many dishes. The tubes of specialty European varieties come in handy for travel or picnics, and pair well with salami and cold meats. We love searching for new mustards and I usually end up with five or six different ones in my fridge at any given time.

TAHINI

Tahini is a paste made from ground sesame seeds. It is an essential ingredient in hummus and I have not found a substitute for it. You can find it at most grocery stores. Once it's open, store it upside down (tightly sealed) in the fridge and shake well before using.

WASABI

Wasabi is a Japanese root much like horseradish. Fierce with an intense bite, it should be used sparingly. If you buy wasabi in powder form, store it in the freezer and make sure you use cold water when you're mixing it into a paste.

Spices and Seeds

CHILI FLAKES

Dried crushed red chili flakes are used at the end of cooking, in tomato sauce recipes or on pizzas, for example, to add a spicy punch.

CORIANDER

Coriander is the seed of the herb we know as cilantro. It is available whole or ground. I personally like whole seeds that I can then grind myself. I usually toast them in a 350°F oven for 4 to 5 minutes then grind them in a spice grinder. They burn easily so keep a close eye. When toasted and ground they are wonderful in curries and Southwestern cuisine.

CURRY POWDER

A reliable pre-made curry powder blend is Madras. The options for homemade blends are endless: they can have as few as 4 spices or a blend of up to 20. Mine is a blend of turmeric, cumin, cloves, mustard seeds, chilies and nutmeg. Curry powders have a short shelf life, only a few months, so don't buy in bulk.

HEMP SEEDS

Hemp seeds are available in most health food stores hulled or whole. The health benefits are abundant so give them a try: they contain all 20 common amino acids and more protein than soy, and are higher in essential fatty acids than any other nut or seed. They add a crunch to breading that I adore; I also like to sprinkle them on salads or add them to smoothies.

MEXICAN OREGANO

Mexican oregano is stronger and less sweet than the Mediterranean oregano that most of us are used to. They're actually two different plants. Not surprisingly, each type is best suited for use in the cuisine of the region where it grows.

MUSTARD SEEDS

Yellow mustard seeds are the ones most commonly used in North American cuisine and are used in most commercial mustards. Dried mustard is finely ground for easy use. Black or brown mustard seeds are generally used in Asian cooking.

SAFFRON

This luxury spice comes from the iris plant and, when activated by heat, adds a deep red coloring to foods. It is a very important ingredient in my Left Coast Seafood Stew. It's expensive, but you only need a little at a time.

SESAME SEEDS

I often use sweet, nutty black and white sesame seeds. They have a short shelf life, so buy them in small quantities and store them in airtight containers in a cool, dry, dark spot.

TURMERIC

This bright orange spice is related to ginger and crops up frequently in curries and mustards. It tastes rather bitter and is often used to provide color rather than taste. It contains an antioxidant called curcumin and is thought to have many beneficial properties.

Oils

Choosing which oil to use depends very much on what you're using it for. Oils with a low smoking point have more limited cooking uses, and are generally more suitable for salad dressings. You should also take into account whether you want the taste of the oil to come through in the finished dish (in which case you're looking for a stronger-flavored oil) or if you want it to blend in with the main ingredients (in which case you want a neutral-flavored oil).

OLIVE OIL

Olive oil of all grades is the current star of our kitchen, stimulating the palette and all senses. It has a lower smoking point than canola oil and I still love to cook with it at lower heats. It's worth spending the extra for a quality product. One ounce a day is supposed to be extremely good for your health. I generally use pure olive oil for cooking and extra virgin for salad dressings, spreads and condiments. My personal favorite is Eleni from the Basil Olive Oil company.

CANOLA OIL

Canola is a neutral oil common in North America. It has a high smoking point and is lower in saturated fats than peanut oil and sunflower oil, among others. Unfortunately, a lot of canola oil seems to have been tainted by GMOs. I always check the label to make sure it says organic and non-GMO to be on the safe side. Grapeseed oil is an excellent substitute but it's usually double the price.

SESAME OIL

This Asian staple is quite strongly flavored and should be used sparingly in sauces and dressings. It has a low smoking point so I tend not to use it much for cooking.

Dairy

MILK

I like to use 2 percent milk, but the recipes in this book will turn out just fine if you prefer to use whole milk, 1 percent or even skim.

BUTTERMILK

This tangy, thick by-product of churned milk is a staple in Southern cooking. You can make a substitute by adding 1 Tbsp of lemon juice or vinegar to 1 cup of milk. Despite the name, it doesn't contain any butter and it's surprisingly low in fat.

CREAM

I use heavy whipping cream with about 36 percent fat, as it does not curdle as easily as a lower-fat cream (for example, regular whipping cream, which is 35 percent fat) or milk.

SOUR CREAM

Sour cream is usually 18–20 percent fat, but you can use low-fat. Crème fraîche is a heavier version of sour cream and can be used as a substitute. (But note that the reverse doesn't hold true.) You can make crème fraîche by adding 1 Tbsp sour cream to 1 cup heavy cream and letting it stand for 12 to 18 hours at room temperature. You can also make a sour cream substitute. My mom in her dieting days would blend low-fat cottage cheese with a dash of milk and lemon and use it for sour cream.

YOGURT

Yogurt, fermented milk with healthy bacteria, has become extremely popular in the past few decades. The recipes in this book use unflavored plain yogurt. Full-fat (about 4 percent) or low-fat are equally fine. Greek yogurt is great for cooking as it is thicker and gives great viscosity to dishes.

BUTTER

I like salted butter myself but in some baking recipes I specify unsalted so that I can control the amount of salt. If you use salted butter, omit the salt from the recipe and add it gradually, tasting as you go along.

EGGS

Free-range organic are my preference and large size is what I use as a measurement for these recipes. Backyard chicken coops are springing up all over, providing fresh eggs daily.

FROMAGE FRAIS

Fromage frais is light, creamy, low in fat and ideal for cooking or using as a spread. You can change its flavor by adding different herbs. My favorite brand is Little Qualicum Cheeseworks, produced here on Vancouver Island. You can substitute mascarpone, ricotta or cream cheese.

HARD AGED CHEESE

Parmesan, pecorino and Asiago are all good-quality hard cheeses. Experiment with substituting these for each other in the recipes in this book.

CHEDDAR CHEESE

Southwestern recipes often call for cheddar, which for me means white in color and medium in flavor. A soft, mild Mexican cheese called queso fresco (Spanish for "fresh cheese") can be used in enchiladas or as a topping for burritos if cheddar is too rich for you.

BLUE CHEESE

Blue cheeses are widely available and cheesemakers across North America are producing some very high-quality varieties. Gorgonzola, roquefort or Stilton tend to substitute well for each other.

GOAT CHEESE

Goat cheese, or chèvre, can be soft or firm, but always has a mild taste. Soft goat cheese is usually sold in logs or disks, and can be plain or flavored with herbs. Firm goat cheese is most familiar to us as feta.

Dry Ingredients

SALT

Kosher salt is what I cook with, and it is what is called for in the recipes unless otherwise specified. Sea salt is great fun to experiment with, from local Vancouver Island varieties to fleur de sel from France, or Himalayan pink or black salts. Their flavor strengths vary though so substitute gradually if you're substituting sea salt for kosher or table salt.

PEPPER

I prefer to grind whole black peppercorns as needed. That's what the recipes in this book require unless otherwise stated. There are some pretty terrific varieties of pepper out there, so be adventurous and do some exploring.

CORNMEAL

Corn is one of those foods that seem to grow under the shadow of GMOs, so I lean toward organic brands like Anita's or Bob's Red Mill. Cornmeal is available coarse ground (for polenta), medium ground (for cornbread) and fine ground (for ultra-crispy fried crusts).

FLOUR

My recipes call for unbleached organic white flour unless otherwise specified. Not all flours are created equal, and white flour and whole wheat flours are not necessarily interchangeable, so follow the recipe instructions. The wrong flour can produce some very disappointing results when you're baking. If someone local mills their own flour, try to buy from them, as flour should be used while extremely fresh. Time in the cupboard is its enemy.

RICE FLOUR

A really nice option for gluten-free, rice flour produces a light, crisp exterior when used for breading for fried foods. I prefer to buy brown rice flour.

DRIED COCONUT

I usually use sweetened shredded coconut, but you can use unsweetened if you prefer. The difference is minimal. If you choose to grate fresh coconut, you can store it in an airtight container for up to 1 week in the fridge or up to 6 months in the freezer.

Rice and Grains

BROWN RICE

Brown rice is a high-fiber grain that comes in short or long varieties. I like its nutty flavor. It takes a little longer to cook but is well worth it from a nutritional point of view. If you haven't tasted brown rice before, you should know that its texture is a little firmer than that of white rice.

SUSHI RICE

This short-grain glutinous rice is available in most grocery stores. If you have access to a Japanese specialty store try the different grades; the supreme is a special treat. Sushi rice should be rinsed well before using. Use a rice cooker to get perfect rice every time (but be sure to measure correctly).

ABORIO RICE

Arborio rice is the Italian short-grain rice used in risotto. During cooking it releases more soluble starch than other types of rice. That's what gives risotto its wonderful creamy texture. Aborio and sushi rice are interchangeable in an emergency as they are both short-grained and starchy.

QUINOA

This versatile South American grain is high in amino acids and protein. I like to rinse it then lightly toast it in the oven before boiling or steaming. Quinoa has a natural coating that tastes bitter. If you don't rinse before cooking, it won't taste good. Note that the seeds are tiny, so use a very fine mesh sieve for rinsing.

Fresh Fruit and Vegetables

GARLIC

Fresh garlic is used extensively throughout this book. I love garlic, and the fact that it has so many health benefits is a bonus. It grows underground and its shoot comes out in the spring. The shoots are called green garlic or garlic scapes, and they're fabulous in soups and sautés. After the garlic has started to mature it forms bulbs, made of the cloves individually cocooned in a papery covering that we're familiar with. Garlic adds something that no other vegetable or spice can, although shallots come close. Chinese garlic is cheaper than domestically grown garlic, but I find it's an inferior product and I stay clear. Local or California all the way.

SHALLOTS

These small, purplish garlic-like onions are classic ingredients in sauces and dressings. Their flavor is mild compared to other onions. If I don't have one on hand I substitute equal parts garlic and red onion.

ONIONS

My rule of thumb is white onions for Southwestern/ Mexican cuisine, yellow for North American and European and red for raw, thinly sliced applications. Some of my favorite varieties are Walla Walla from Washington, 1015s from Texas and Vidalias from Georgia. Sizes vary widely, so take that into account while preparing recipes. Generally speaking, medium is a safe bet.

POTATOES

While I tend to lean heavily on Yukon Golds or yellow flesh for their versatility, I find russets better for gnocchi (thanks to their mealy texture) and early nuggets (which are waxy) perfect for steaming. Heritage potatoes are sprouting up all over and I recommend you look for them at your local farmers' market. The purple and blues are especially nice. I think they steam better than they roast.

MIXED GREENS

Mixed salad greens can be a mixture of whatever leaves you like. Mesclun mix made its way onto our plates a few decades ago and is still around. Try it with kale, chard, beet tops, spinach and arugula for a fortified salad.

ARUGULA

Often referred to as rocket, this peppery leaf is amazing in salads and pestos, and as a topping for pizza.

WATERCRESS

Grown in water, this natural super-food loaded with minerals and vitamins is great in pestos, salads, soups and sauces. It's thought to have antibacterial properties and may help in the treatment of health complaints.

CUCUMBER

The recipes in this book work with garden, English or lemon cucumbers, unless specified otherwise. The thickness of skin varies between varieties, but as a general rule of thumb: garden cucumbers are tough-skinned; English are medium; lemon are thin-skinned. If you are concerned about peeling or not peeling cucumbers, I generally find that peeling just half of the cucumber (meaning peeling every other strip, to create a striped effect) gets around the issue!

BERRIES

Blueberries, strawberries and blackberries can often be substituted for one another. Berries freeze extremely well if you flash-freeze them by placing them in a single layer on a baking pan until completely frozen then transferring them to freezer bags (or even better, vacuum-pack them). They'll keep frozen for up to a year. The recipes in this book generally call for fresh berries, but frozen can work really well. Simply thaw frozen berries and strain off any excess juice before using. (And don't underestimate how long it takes berries to thaw.)

GINGER

I use three different types of ginger. Fresh ginger is a knobby hand-sized root with light tan skin and a light yellow flesh. It should be clean, unwrinkled and free of mold. You generally peel off the outer skin before using. If it is greenish-blue inside it is old and should not be used. I prefer to grate or finely mince it as needed when cooking. You can store it in the fridge or freezer, but it's better to buy it when you're planning to use it.

Fresh ginger can be used in curries, sauces and dressings, or added to smoothies or tea. It has been known to aid in digestion and sore throats. Dried ginger is used mostly for baking and should not be substituted for fresh. Crystallized ginger is the candied form. We like it in cookies.

Canned Vegetables

CHIPOTLE CHILIES

Smoked jalapeños are available dried or canned in adobo sauce. I specify canned for most of my recipes and they're the more readily available option. I purée a whole can at once to make life easier with less clean-up. They'll keep for up to 1 week if stored in an airtight container in the fridge.

DRIED CHILIES

Dried chilies are a favorite of mine—they add so much depth and flavor to Mexican cookery. Wear gloves when handling anchos, guajillos and habaneros. Lightly toast then rehydrate the chilies in hot water before using. (You can also grind the dried chilies if you prefer.)

GREEN CHILIES

Roasted, seeded Anaheim chilies are available chopped or whole in cans. You can use them as a substitute for fresh roasted poblanos in soups and sauces, although they're a bit milder. I don't use canned for *chiles rellenos*, but it is possible.

CANNED TOMATOES

For pizzas I like Italian San Marzano tomatoes. They are a beautiful deep red color, and have a full-bodied taste. Otherwise, I've been happy with Muir Glen Organic tomatoes. I prefer canned tomatoes to tomatoes out of season any day.

FIRE-ROASTED TOMATOES

Buying fire-roasted tomatoes in cans saves you charring/roasting your own. These are a great choice for soups and recipes where Southwestern flavors dominate.

ROASTED RED PEPPERS

Buying roasted red peppers in cans saves you roasting and peeling your own. I always rinse mine before using.

BEANS

I will always choose to cook my beans from dried if time allows but in a pinch canned are an acceptable substitute. Just rinse and drain them before using. One cup of uncooked, dried beans is the equivalent of 3–4 cups cooked beans (so, ½ cup dried beans will give the equivalent of a 15 oz can), although it varies slightly according to the type of bean. I keep pintos, navy, black, garbanzo and cannellini beans, both dried and canned, on hand. Dried beans should be kept in airtight containers and stored in a cool, dry, dark place. Cooked beans can be kept in airtight containers in the fridge for up to 5 days or in the freezer for up to 6 months.

OLIVES

What's the difference between black and green olives? Black are ripened and green are not. Both types go through a process of brining or curing, which give them flavor profiles. I like to keep a wide variety on hand for impromptu get-togethers. My personal favorites are Agrinion, green cracked and Kalamata from the Basil Olive Oil company (of course!).

Breakfast

SoBo Biscuits 37

Flaxseed and Ginger Pancakes 38

Strawberry Lemon Scones 41

Blueberry Muffins 42

Granola 45

Broiled Grapefruit with Honey and Coconut 46

Huevos Rancheros 49

Spot Prawn Benny 53

Texas Egg Bake 55

Morel Mushroom Scramble 56

Florentine Breakfast Pizza 59

Breakfast Sandwich with Smoked Tuna Bacon 61

SoBo Biscuits

Biscuits have been a part of my life for as long as I can remember. I even landed my first real, full-time cooking job on a private yacht in Florida by understanding the art of making biscuits.

2 cups flour, plus extra for dusting the work surface

1 Tbsp plus 1 tsp baking powder

1 Tbsp sugar

1 tsp salt

½ tsp cream of tartar

½ cup very cold butter, cubed

¾ cup milk

Makes 8 biscuits

Preheat the oven to 400°F. Lightly grease a baking sheet, or line it with parchment paper.

In a large bowl, sift together the flour, baking powder, sugar, salt and cream of tartar. Combine the butter into the dry ingredients by using two forks or a pastry cutter. Work quickly to blend the butter before it starts to soften and melt. The consistency you are looking for is like wet sand, with very small pea-like pieces.

Slowly add the milk, stirring with a wooden spoon to soften the dough. The dough will be slightly sticky. Turn it onto a lightly floured surface and knead 11–12 times. The dough will get nice and soft, but don't overknead or it will become tough.

Roll out the dough into a rectangle about 1 inch thick and cut it into eight pieces. I like to cut my biscuits into squares so I use all the dough. If a round shape is more to your liking, use a Mason jar top or a cookie cutter. You'll need to reroll the dough in order to use it all if you go for a round shape.

Place the biscuits on the prepared baking sheet about 1 inch apart from each other and bake for 10 to 15 minutes or until golden.

Flaxseed and Ginger Pancakes

These ginger pancakes were first part of our ranch life in Texas when we did breakfast seven days a week for our guests. We were always striving to do something different from the basic buttermilk or blueberry pancake. Molasses is a very familiar flavor in the south, but flaxseeds aren't. I love their crunchy texture, and their health benefits aren't so bad, either. Pancakes are our weekend treat, just as I imagine they are for lots of families who celebrate Saturday mornings together. At our house I make the mix and then let Artie take over!

1 cup flour

1 cup whole wheat flour

¼ cup whole golden or brown flaxseeds

2 Tbsp baking powder

2 tsp ground ginger

½ tsp ground allspice

½ tsp ground cinnamon

½ tsp salt

1 egg plus 1 egg white

2 ¼ cups milk

3 Tbsp butter

2 Tbsp molasses

Cooking spray or 1 tsp canola oil

Makes 10 pancakes (serves 4–6)

Combine both flours with the flaxseeds, baking powder, spices and salt in a large mixing bowl and incorporate them using a wire whisk. In a separate mixing bowl, combine the egg, egg white, milk, butter and molasses and whisk until frothy, about 2 minutes.

Make a well in the center of the dry mix, then pour in the wet ingredients and mix with a wooden spoon until fully incorporated (it's fine if there are still some lumps).

Spray a medium-sized frying pan or pancake griddle with cooking spray, or add a few drops of canola oil, and heat the frying pan over medium heat. Pour ¼ cup of batter onto the frying pan for each pancake. Cook for 2 to 3 minutes, or until bubbles form on top and the edges start to crinkle and dry, then flip the pancakes over and cook the second side for another 2 to 3 minutes.

....

COOK'S NOTE: *These pancakes are rich and dense, and they cook a little darker than a traditional buttermilk pancake. They also have a tendency to burn easily due to the sugar content of the molasses, so keep an eye on them! Caramelized sliced apples or pears are a welcome addition to these pancakes. Just slice a few apples or pears and toss them with 1 Tbsp sugar and 1 Tbsp butter in a hot frying pan until tender, then scatter on top of the pancakes.*

Strawberry Lemon Scones

I can't take credit for this recipe. It's from our pastry chef, Jen Scott, and is so easy to make! She makes some of the most delicious baked goods I have ever tasted—homey yet elegant, which is just what I'm looking for. You can substitute blueberries, blackberries, raspberries or currants for the strawberries. On special occasions we even add a cup of white chocolate chunks or chips.

2 eggs

2 cups flour plus ¼ cup for kneading

3 Tbsp sugar

1 Tbsp baking powder

½ tsp salt

½ cup very cold butter, cubed

½ cup milk

¼ cup lemon juice (1 large lemon)

1 cup strawberries, stemmed and sliced

Zest of 1 lemon

1 Tbsp icing sugar (optional)

Makes 10 scones

Preheat the oven to 425°F. Line a baking sheet with parchment paper.

Beat the eggs in a small bowl and set aside. Combine the 2 cups of flour with the sugar, baking powder and salt in a large bowl and mix thoroughly with a wire whisk.

Start to incorporate the butter into the dry ingredients using a pastry cutter, two forks or a food processor (use the steel blade and pulsing function). For a tender, layered pastry, work quickly to blend the butter before it starts to soften and melt. You want the mixture to resemble wet sand. Once it is there, pour in half of the beaten egg, and the milk and lemon juice. Stir with a wooden spoon until the mixture is sticky and then fold in the strawberries and lemon zest

Flour a board or countertop, and gently knead the dough 10–12 times. You are looking for a soft dough. It should not be too sticky (that means too much liquid) and it should not be separating (that means too much flour). If you need more flour or milk just add a scant amount to get the desired result.

Roll out the dough into a rectangle about ½ inch thick (flouring the surface as needed). Cut out 10 of your desired shapes. I prefer to cut triangles or squares for zero waste, as using a round cookie cutter will mean you end up with excess trim that you have to reroll.

Place the shapes on the prepared baking sheet about 1 inch apart from each other. Use a pastry brush to brush the top of the dough with the remaining beaten egg for a shiny finish. (You can opt to add 1 Tbsp of icing sugar to the egg if you like added sweetness.)

Bake in the oven for 12 to 14 minutes or until golden.

Fresh Strawberries

When the strawberries start popping out at Nanoose Edibles Organic Farm (see page 96) we get giddy with anticipation. Every week as the season progresses, we try to judge the best time to do our big buy. Some weeks we think the berries cannot get any better and we freeze hundreds of pounds, then—bam!—the next week they are even sweeter! So we do another 300 pounds. This goes on and on until one day Jen and I look at each other and say, "I guess that's it." Somehow we end up with 1,000 pounds in the freezer every year. But it works, because in fall, winter and spring, we thaw and roast them (see page 237) for scones, desserts and smoothies.

Blueberry Muffins

We use about 1,000 pounds of blueberries a year at SoBo. They are mostly used for compotes and sauces in the restaurant, but a good deal get gobbled up by our kids. They love to eat the berries frozen, chomping them like popcorn. And we're lucky enough to have one of the country's best organic blueberry farms—Avalon Farms—located just over two hours away in Port Alberni.

2 cups flour

½ cup sugar

2 ½ tsp baking powder

¾ tsp salt

1 egg

¾ cup milk

⅓ cup canola oil

1 cup blueberries

Makes 10–12 muffins (depending on how big you like them)

Preheat the oven to 400°F. Line a muffin pan with paper liners or grease the cups with baking spray or a lightly oiled paper towel.

Combine the flour, sugar, baking powder and salt in a large mixing bowl and incorporate them using a wire whisk. In a separate bowl, combine the egg, milk and oil, and beat with a wire whisk until frothy.

Make a well in the center of the dry mix, then pour in the wet ingredients and mix with a wooden spoon until just incorporated. Fold in the blueberries gently.

Use a spoon or an ice cream scoop to fill the muffin cups to three-quarters full. Bake for 20 to 25 minutes or until a wooden skewer inserted into the center comes out clean.

. . . .

COOK'S NOTE: *I like using an ice cream scoop for making muffins and cookies because it creates a smooth-crowned top. It also allows for easy measuring so that all the muffins or cookies come out the same size.*

Cathy and Kerry McDonald
PORT ALBERNI, BC

When you're driving across Vancouver Island to get to Tofino, just before the winding road that leads you through the mountains, you will reach the small town of Port Alberni. Set at the head of a long ocean inlet, Port Alberni was once known mostly as a mill and logging town, but the Alberni Valley is also home to some of Vancouver Island's best growing land. That's where you'll find Cathy and Kerry McDonald of Avalon Farm, who supply SoBo with organic blueberries and spot prawns.

Cathy and Kerry are amazing people—full of passion and love. We became friends with them in 2010, when they stopped into the restaurant with some of the plumpest, tastiest blueberries I'd ever seen. Dedicated to organic farming and sustainable fishing, they've been a welcome addition to the SoBo family. We buy all the berries they can sell us, but they have to leave a few for other people!

"It's great that more and more people are acknowledging real food and what it takes to put it on a plate," says Kerry. "I'm inspired by all of the people who are willing to put in the hard work that's needed to change the current food system, so that we can all be healthier and happier. For me, it's gratifying that we get to watch, and help, Nature do her work through the seasons. And then, later, a diner gets to linger over the burst of flavor, texture and vitality that's evident in each bite of the ingredients we produce. That's the final culmination of the work we do."

Granola

We sell granola by the pound at SoBo and to say we've made thousands of pounds of it would be an understatement. I can't recall how this recipe came about but it is constantly evolving according to what dried fruits and nuts are available. We also sometimes change the honey to maple syrup. Granola makes a great kid's snack, a hearty breakfast or a late-night dessert with vanilla yogurt. Sometimes I even toss it into cookie dough. It also freezes well and makes a wonderful hostess gift.

2 cups rolled oats

¼ cup shredded sweetened or unsweetened coconut

¼ cup mix of pecans, cashews and pumpkin seeds

¼ cup canola oil

¼ cup honey

1 Tbsp ground cinnamon

1 tsp grated nutmeg

1 tsp salt

¼ cup mix of chopped dried apricots, raisins, dates or goji berries

Makes 2 lb (serves 4–6)

Preheat the oven to 325°F.

Spread the rolled oats on a cookie sheet and toast them in the oven for 15 to 20 minutes. Toast the coconut on a separate baking sheet for 5 minutes. Remove both baking sheets from the oven and set aside to cool. Turn the oven down to 200°F.

In a large bowl, mix together the oats, nuts and seeds, oil, honey, cinnamon, nutmeg and salt until well combined. Spread out on a cookie sheet and bake in the oven until lightly browned, about 30 minutes. Remove from the oven and set aside to cool, about 30 minutes. This will allow the granola to clump together.

Once cooled, transfer to a large bowl, breaking up any larger pieces. Add the toasted coconut and dried fruit, tossing well to combine.

....

COOK'S NOTE: *Fruit, seed and nut combinations are very flexible. Granola is a personal thing, and I encourage you to make this recipe your own by experimenting with different combinations. If you don't like coconut, just add more fruit, seeds or nuts. This granola can be stored in a tightly sealed container for up to 2 weeks.*

Broiled Grapefruit
with Honey and Coconut

This is an excellent sweet and tart way to dress up a Sunday brunch, or serve these as a dessert if you don't want something rich or heavy. I'm a big fan of Texas ruby red grapefruits but pinks also work well. There are many interesting varieties of honey on the market these days, so feel free to experiment with different flavors. I love buckwheat, lavender or wildflower!

4 ruby red grapefruits

½ cup honey

½ cup shredded sweetened
or unsweetened coconut

¼ cup Grand Marnier

Serves 8 (½ grapefruit per serving)

Preheat the oven to 450°F, or to the broil setting if your stove has one. Line a baking sheet with parchment paper.

Slice the grapefruits in half. Run a knife around the outside of the fruit to separate it from the skin, and then between the sections. This makes for easier eating and creates pockets for the honey and Grand Marnier to slide into.

Place the halves, cut side up, on the prepared baking sheet. Drizzle the honey overtop, then sprinkle each half with 2 Tbsp coconut and 1 Tbsp Grand Marnier. Broil or bake for 5 minutes, or until the grapefruits are hot and the coconut is golden brown.

. . . .

COOK'S NOTE: *There's a fine line between broiling and burning. Keep a close eye on the grapefruits while they're cooking. If you do not have a broiler, baking at a very high heat will produce equally delicious results. If you prefer not to have alcohol, just leave out the Grand Marnier.*

Huevos Rancheros

Huevos Rancheros ("rancher's eggs") is a very popular breakfast dish in Texas, and I made it a staple at Cibolo Creek Ranch. You can scramble the eggs instead of frying them, and they're great topped with sliced avocado. I was proud to have this recipe featured in the June 1999 issue of *Food & Wine* magazine. Note that the salsa is made before the eggs! (And the beans take 2 hours to prepare.)

Roasted Tomato Salsa

3 cloves garlic, skins on

1 large sweet onion, sliced into 5–6 intact disks (each ½ inch thick)

5 plum tomatoes, whole

½ cup canned chipotle chilies in adobo sauce

½ cup fresh cilantro

2 tsp salt

Makes 2 cups

Eggs

¼ cup vegetable oil

8 small soft corn tortillas (about 6 inches diameter)

1 ½ cups shredded cheddar cheese

2 Tbsp butter

8 eggs

Pinto Beans (page 213)

1 avocado, sliced

Serves 4

Preheat the oven to 350°F.

For the salsa, heat a large cast iron frying pan over medium-high heat. Add the garlic and cook until slightly softened and the skins are just turning black all over. Remove the garlic and set aside to cool. Add the onion slices to the same frying pan, charring on both sides, 2 to 3 minutes for each side.

Remove the onions from the frying pan and set aside. Add the tomatoes to the frying pan and char their skins, about 7 minutes. Remove from the frying pan and set aside with the garlic and onion.

Peel the cooled garlic and transfer to a food processor or blender. Add the garlic, onions, tomatoes, chipotles, cilantro and salt, and pulse just until the mixture is still a little chunky.

Heat the oil in a nonstick frying pan over medium-high heat. Using tongs, dip both sides of each tortilla into the hot oil until just softened, about 5 seconds for each side. Let any oil drip back into the frying pan. Place the tortillas on paper towel to soak up any excess oil.

Spoon 1 ½ Tbsp cheese onto each tortilla and roll up tightly. Arrange the tortillas side by side, seam side down, in an 8- × 8-inch or 9- × 9-inch casserole dish. Top the tortillas with the salsa and sprinkle the remaining cheese overtop. Bake for about 10 minutes or until the salsa and tortillas are warmed through and the cheese is melted.

Heat the butter in a nonstick frying pan and fry the eggs sunny-side up for 3 to 4 minutes each. Arrange two tortillas on each plate and top with two fried eggs. Serve with the pinto beans on the side and garnish with avocado slices.

Spring

Tofino starts to buzz again with the onset of spring. The surfers return with wild stories from exotic places; the local fishing fleets shrug off their deep sleep and get back to work; thousands of gray whales—babies in tow—return and say hello on their way to Alaska; the number of tourists begins to noticeably swell; and the town gossip, dreams and doubts turn to ingredients: "Are the salmon going to run heavy this year?" "I can't wait for the first spot prawns!" "Do you know where the good nettle patches are?" Spring is a season of renewal and anticipation everywhere, but it just feels more concentrated and exciting in Tofino, as if it's never happened before.

Spot Prawn Benny

The words "eggs Benedict" sweep me away to a time when my girlfriends and I would head to the fanciest local hotel (The Breakers in West Palm Beach, Florida) and treat ourselves to champagne and eggs Benedict. There are many ways to make this popular brunch item, but our juicy, local spot prawns make this version my favorite. Sorrel is even more abundant than prawns in Tofino, and it adds a natural lemony flavor that goes a long way in a Benny.

4 SoBo Biscuits (page 37)

Classic Hollandaise (page 54)

½ cup white vinegar

8 eggs

2 Tbsp olive oil

16 spot prawns, peeled and deveined (frozen and thawed shrimp works equally well)

Salt

8 leaves fresh sorrel

4 sprigs fresh dill

Serves 4

Prepare the SoBo biscuits and the hollandaise sauce.

Preheat the oven to 400°F. Line an ovenproof pan with paper towel.

Fill a heavy-bottomed saucepan with water and bring to a steady simmer (so there is movement but the water is not boiling), then add the vinegar.

Carefully crack one egg at a time into the vinegar-seasoned water. Do not overcrowd the eggs. I usually do two at a time so I can keep track of the cooking time for each egg. After 2 minutes, remove the eggs with a slotted spoon and place them in the prepared pan. Keep the eggs lightly heated in the oven.

If the SoBo biscuits have cooled, warm them in the center of the oven for 3 minutes.

Heat the olive oil in a frying pan over high heat. Lightly salt the prawns and then cook them for no longer than 30 to 45 seconds on each side—prawns cook very quickly and are easy to overcook. They will turn a bright orange or red when ready.

To assemble each Benny, split a biscuit in half and place each one side by side in the center of a plate. Lay a leaf of sorrel on top of each half then top with two prawns per side, followed by one egg per side. Top with hollandaise and finish with a sprig of fresh dill.

continued on next page

Classic Hollandaise

4 egg yolks

2 Tbsp water

1 cup cold butter, cubed

2 Tbsp lemon juice (1 medium lemon)

Pinch cayenne pepper

Salt

Makes 1 ½ cups

Fill the bottom of a double boiler (or saucepan) with enough water to boil for 10 minutes without running dry. The water should not touch the bottom of the upper part of the double boiler (or stainless steel bowl). You are trying to evenly, gently heat the upper part of the boiler. If the water touches the bottom, the hollandaise is likely to scorch or curdle. If you don't have a double boiler you can create one by setting a stainless steel bowl on top of a medium-sized saucepan.

In the upper part of the double boiler, whisk the egg yolks and water until frothy. Continue whisking constantly yet gently and the eggs will start to increase in volume.

At this point, start adding the butter cubes one at a time, continuing to whisk. As one cube melts, add another, until they are all incorporated. If the sauce starts to get too thick just add 1 tsp water. When the sauce has completely emulsified, add the lemon juice and cayenne. Season to taste.

Once ready, it is best to serve the sauce right away. You can hold it for up to 2 hours, but it is tricky to keep it warm without it "breaking." I usually hold it in the upper part of the boiler, whisking every so often. If your oven is on, you could also place the pot in the center of the stovetop, and the rising heat from the oven will warm it.

Perfect Hollandaise

Training at the Culinary Institute of America (CIA) gave me a very strong appreciation of the classics. Once you understand a traditional cooking method or recipe, you can branch out and create your own versions. This hollandaise is mine, and I encourage you to play with it once you've mastered it. One of my favorite variations is to add ¼ cup of Salsa Verde (page 141) and a little cream or pico de gallo to the finished sauce. While a lot of cooks like clarified butter for hollandaise I really prefer the taste of fresh butter—I find clarified butter greasy and far too rich.

Texas Egg Bake

This is what happens when a quiche meets a soufflé. While working at Cibolo Creek Ranch in Texas we sometimes had to feed 30 people a hearty breakfast all at once. My solution was invariably an egg bake. I could put the chilies and cheese together the night before and in the morning I could just whip the eggs and cream, pour them over the chilies and cheese, cover the whole thing with aluminum foil and then pop it in the oven. It's ready in an hour.

1 Tbsp canola oil

One 4 oz can diced green chilies, or ½ cup roasted poblano or Anaheim chilies

2 cups grated cheddar cheese

5 eggs

1 cup whipping cream

½ tsp salt

½ tsp pepper

Roasted Corn and Potato Hash (page 217)

Serves 4

Preheat the oven to 400°F. Coat a deep 8- × 8-inch or 9- × 9-inch ovenproof dish with the oil.

Spread the chilies and cheese across the bottom of the prepared dish.

In a blender, mix the eggs, cream, salt and pepper on high for 1 minute or until frothy. Pour this cream mixture over the chilies and cheese, cover with aluminum foil and bake for 45 minutes. Remove the foil, and bake for a further 15 minutes. The egg bake will be almost soufflé-like when it comes out of the oven. If it is not, bake for a further 15 minutes.

While the eggs are baking prepare the roasted corn and potato hash.

To serve, divide the egg bake between four plates and add a side of the hash. Warm SoBo Biscuits (page 37) are lovely with this recipe, or sometimes I like to wrap up the eggs in a soft corn tortilla and eat them like you would a burrito.

Morel Mushroom Scramble

The first time I ever ate a morel mushroom I was working at the Old Chatham Sheepherding Company Inn in upstate New York. Walking across the lawn one day I saw this one lonesome, weird-looking mushroom popping up out of the ground. I asked the chef, Melissa Kelly, if it was edible. "Haven't you ever tried a morel?" she asked, surprised. Embarrassed, I told her I hadn't, so she took it, sliced it up and sautéed it in butter with a single whipped egg and a hint of chive. To this day, it remains the best mushroom experience I've ever had!

3 Tbsp butter

5 fresh morel mushrooms, cleaned and sliced (see sidebar page 149)

6 eggs, at room temperature

½ tsp salt

Pepper

½ cup fromage frais (this is a French fresh cheese, and you can use soft goat cheese or mascarpone if you prefer)

¼ cup minced chives

Serves 4

Melt 2 Tbsp of the butter in a frying pan over high heat, and as it melts toss in the morels (if you wait for the butter to melt completely you may end up burning it). Toss or stir the mushrooms continuously as they cook, about 4 minutes. You want a bit of crispiness and for them to be thoroughly cooked through. Remove from the frying pan and set aside. Wipe out the frying pan with paper towel and return to the stovetop with the heat turned off.

In a bowl, whisk together the eggs until they're very frothy, about 2 minutes. Add the salt and pepper and whisk again.

Reheat the frying pan over medium-high heat and add the remaining 1 Tbsp butter, distributing it evenly as it melts. Pour in the eggs. Cook for 30 to 60 seconds to allow the eggs to set. Then, with a rubber spatula, start moving the egg mixture toward the center of the pan and lightly turning it over. Continue moving and folding the eggs until they are soft, fluffy and cooked to your liking. Fold in the mushrooms, cheese and chives and serve right away.

Scrambling Eggs

One of the things I ask prospective cooks to do for me when they apply for a job is to scramble an egg. You'd be amazed at how many people mess it up. Ensure your frying pan is well heated before the eggs go in, but not too hot or they will cook too quickly and scorch. Always push your eggs around in the pan once the base has set.

Florentine Breakfast Pizza

Back in the early '90s, Artie and I managed The Lodge at Fossil Rim, which is located in the middle of a wildlife center just outside Glen Rose, Texas. Many of the guests were families with children who would leave at the crack of dawn every morning for a game drive to view rhinos, giraffes, antelopes and such. They'd all be hungry upon their return—and we know how fussy little kids can be—so when we introduced pizza for breakfast we looked like heroes. The kids devoured it and the grown-ups loved it, too. (Note that the pizza dough has to sit for 2 hours before it can be cooked.)

Pizza Dough (page 60)

2 Tbsp olive oil

2 lb spinach or baby spinach, stems removed (about 12 handfuls)

½ tsp salt

8 eggs

2 cups ricotta cheese

2 cups shredded mozzarella

2 large tomatoes (plum or beefsteak), thinly sliced into ¼-inch wheels, halved

Makes 2 pizzas (serves 6)

Preheat the oven to 450°F. Prepare the pizza dough and set aside.

Heat the olive oil in a large frying pan over medium-high heat. Add all the spinach, turning often with tongs until wilted, about 2 minutes. Season with the salt. Remove the spinach from the frying pan and let it sit in a strainer for 10 minutes over the sink. Using tongs or your hands, squeeze the excess moisture from the leaves.

In a blender or food processor, whip the spinach, eggs and ricotta for 2 minutes or until doubled in volume. The mixture will be frothy.

Roll half of the pizza dough directly onto a baking sheet, or into a 12-inch deep-dish "Chicago-style" pizza pan (it can be either round or rectangular). The dough should hang over the edges of the pan so you can pinch up the edges to create a "dish" effect.

Lay a piece of parchment paper on top of the dough and place a pan of equal or similar size on top to weigh the dough down (you can also use baking beans). This is a blind baking method that will ensure the crust is thoroughly baked. Bake for 6 minutes. Repeat with the remaining dough for the second pizza crust.

To top the pizzas, sprinkle the mozzarella evenly over the bases. Very slowly pour the egg mixture on top of the mozzarella, being careful not to overflow the brim. Scatter the tomato slices on top of the pizzas.

Turn the oven down to 400°F and bake for 15 to 20 minutes or until the eggs are completely set. Remove from the oven and let the pizzas rest for a few minutes, then slice and serve.

continued on next page

Pizza Dough

1 Tbsp honey

1 cup warm water (warm enough to touch, but not too hot, about 110°F)

1 Tbsp active dry yeast

1 ½ cups flour

1 cup whole wheat flour

½ cup cornmeal

¼ cup olive oil

½ tsp salt

Makes two 12-inch pizza bases

In a medium-sized bowl, stir the honey into the warm water until it is dissolved. Gently sprinkle in the yeast, stirring until incorporated. The yeast mixture should be a light tan and have no lumps—this is crucial for a light and crispy pizza base. Cover the mixture with plastic wrap and let sit in a warm, draft-free place for 10 minutes or until a puffy foam forms on top of the mixture. If the foam is not forming, toss it out and start over. It means the water was either too cold or too hot, which stops the yeast from activating.

Combine both flours with the cornmeal, olive oil and salt in a large mixing bowl. Add the yeast mixture and stir until a smooth ball forms. You don't want it to be too sticky or too dry. It should be elastic and almost shiny. You may need to add a little more flour (if it's too wet) or water (if it's too dry) depending on the consistency before you knead the dough.

Turn the dough onto a floured surface and knead until it becomes smooth and elastic. It is almost impossible to overknead this dough. If you have a good mixer with a dough hook, this is a great time to take advantage of it. I personally love to knead by hand, but if you're multitasking the machine is a super option.

Transfer the dough to a lightly oiled bowl, turning the dough once to coat all the sides with oil. Cover the bowl with plastic wrap and a kitchen towel, and set it in a warm, draft-free spot to let the dough rise for an hour or two until it doubles in size. Punch the dough down to remove all the air bubbles. It is now ready to be used.

About Pizza Dough

This is a very basic pizza dough. The yield depends on how thin you like your pizza. For this recipe I'd recommend rolling it to create two pizza bases, but it could stretch to three. It can be punched down twice if rising occurs before you're ready to use it. You can also prepare it in advance and store in a sealed plastic bag in the fridge for up to 24 hours or in the freezer for 3 months. If you are using the dough after it has been frozen or refrigerated, allow it to reach room temperature before continuing with the recipe.

Breakfast Sandwich
with Smoked Tuna Bacon

When SoBo was a food truck we had fish and chicken but no red meat. It is the way I eat at home and since the West Coast has such an abundance of fresh seafood, why would I even bother with pork, lamb or beef? Well, it turned out that people really love their bacon so we came up with items that smelled and tasted bacon-like. Tuna bacon was the most popular, especially in this easy-to-prepare breakfast sandwich. Now I can hear you all saying, "Tuna bacon? Ew!" It might sound strange, but it's delicious. You just have to source a high-quality smoked tuna.

4 SoBo Biscuits (page 37)

8 thin slices smoked albacore tuna

2 Tbsp butter

4 eggs

¼ tsp salt

4 Tbsp shredded cheddar cheese

1 Tbsp mayonnaise

8 leaves fresh spinach

1 avocado, sliced

2 Tbsp Pickled Jalapeños (page 255) (these are optional but really add a nice kick)

Serves 4

Prepare the SoBo biscuits.

Preheat the oven to 275°F. Line a baking sheet with parchment paper.

Place the tuna slices on the prepared baking sheet and bake for 20 minutes. This is to dry the tuna out before you fry it, and it should give it a texture almost like jerky, but not as chewy. Remove the tuna from the oven and turn up the heat to 400°F.

In a nonstick, medium-sized frying pan, heat 1 Tbsp of the butter over medium-high heat. Lay out the tuna slices in the pan just as you would if you were cooking traditional bacon. Turn the slices after 1 to 2 minutes, and fry the other side for 1 to 2 minutes more. The tuna will crisp up very quickly so be careful. Remove from the pan and set aside. Turn the heat off but keep the pan on the stovetop.

Slice the biscuits in half and toast them in the oven for about 4 minutes while preparing the eggs.

Heat the remaining butter in the same pan used for the tuna, over a low heat this time. Gently crack the eggs one by one into the frying pan and season with salt. Let the eggs fry slowly over low heat so they will be tender and less greasy.

When the whites have set, gently flip the eggs over and turn off the heat. There will be enough heat already in the pan to complete the cooking process. Top each egg with 1 Tbsp cheese and keep them in the pan until the cheese starts to melt.

To build each sandwich, spread the bottom half of each biscuit with mayonnaise and top with a few leaves of spinach, then two slices of tuna, one egg and three avocado slices (and some pickled jalapeños if desired). Top with the other half of the biscuit and serve.

Soups

Wild Nettle and Sorrel Soup 65

Roasted Sunchoke and Leek Soup 66

Vegan Yam and Coconut Soup 67

Surfer Noodle Soup 68

Smoked Salmon Chowder 71

Caribbean Geoduck Chowder 72

Black Bean Soup with *Pico de Gallo* 73

Aztec Bean Soup 75

Heritage Squash and Poblano Soup 76

French Green Lentil Soup and Roasted Shiitake Soup 79

Health in a Bowl 80

Roasted Winter Vegetable Soup 83

Carl and Joe Martin

TOFINO, BC

Carl (pictured) and Joe Martin were born and raised on Meares Island, just across the harbor from Tofino. Their father, Chief Robert Martin of the Tla-o-qui-aht First Nation, passed his traditional knowledge to his sons—everything from the creation stories of the area's animals to how to pick the right cedar tree for a dugout canoe. My 52nd birthday present was a feast table that had been cut from the trim of a canoe that the Martin brothers had built—a perfect, solid red cedar slab, 15 feet long and 3 feet wide.

These days, Carl and Joe provide us with local forage foods from the rainforests of their ancestral territory. The West Coast is renowned for its wild seafood—as it deserves to be—but the land also provides some incredible native plants that people here have incorporated into their cooking for many thousands of years.

Depending on the season, they'll bring us nettles, wild onions, seaweed, huckleberries, blackberries or salal berries. I see at least one of them every day through most of the year. They bring me raw ingredients and I turn those ingredients into meals that sustain them for the hard work they do.

As I write this, Joe is up on Sutton Pass with a downed tree, carving out another beautiful dugout canoe, and his brother will shortly be by with a bag of nettles. Both of them, thankfully, are passing their wealth of skill and knowledge on to their own children, so we can trust that the culture of our coast will carry on.

Wild Nettle and Sorrel Soup

Nettles peeking out of the ground are one of the first sure signs of early spring here on the West Coast. They're nature's way of waking us up gently with a healing, cleansing, calcium-rich treat, right when we need it most. Because nettles have stinging hairs, most people handle them with garden gloves or tongs. I'm lucky, as my hands respond well to them. After a long day of cooking on the line, nettles actually help relieve pain from any sore joints in my hands. Don't tell anyone, but sometimes I take the blanching water home to give my feet a good soak! Our main nettle foragers are the wise and gifted Martin brothers, Carl and Joe, of the Tla-o-qui-aht First Nation. They harvest nettles on their property, which is located on a small island just outside Tofino's harbor.

2 lb fresh wild nettle leaves (about 16 cups)

6 Tbsp salt

½ cup olive oil

2 large leeks, whites only, sliced

8 stalks celery, diced small

¼ cup minced garlic (10–12 cloves)

4 cups Vegetable Stock (page 250)

1 Yukon Gold potato, diced medium

½ cup Roasted Garlic (page 252)

2 tsp Tabasco sauce

¼ tsp fresh thyme leaves

½ lb fresh sorrel leaves (about 4 cups)

¼ cup lemon juice (1 large lemon)

Pepper

Serves 4–6

See photo on page 6

To blanch the nettles, bring 4 quarts of water to a boil in a large stockpot and add 4 Tbsp of the salt. Using tongs, lower the nettles into the boiling water, stir and cook until tender, 4 to 5 minutes. Strain the nettles (but save the hot nettle water to soak your feet in!) and transfer them to a large bowl filled with ice-cold water for 1 to 2 minutes. This will shock the nettles and help them retain their deep green color. Drain the nettles again and set aside.

Heat the olive oil in a medium-sized saucepan over medium-high heat, and sauté the leeks, celery and minced garlic until they are translucent. Add the stock, potatoes, roasted garlic, Tabasco, thyme and remaining 2 Tbsp salt. Simmer for 20 minutes, or until the potatoes are soft. Add the blanched nettles, fresh sorrel leaves and lemon juice and stir to incorporate. Use an immersion blender or a food processor to blend the soup until smooth and velvety. Season to taste with salt and pepper.

Roasted Sunchoke and Leek Soup

One day a local woman named Jocelyne drove up to my back door and offered me a big bag of sunchokes. They were so fresh I bought them gladly. As she was leaving, she turned to me with a puzzled expression and asked, "Why don't you harvest your own?" I looked back at her blankly. "What do you mean?" I asked. "Well, the garden in your parking lot is full of them!" she said, pointing out the door. My eyes must have opened wide, because she went out back, got on her knees and dug with her hands under what I thought was just a dead sunflower stalk. A minute later she was holding up a perfect sunchoke. I had no idea! Now our gardener knows to bring them into the kitchen for us, but I still buy them from Jocelyne out of gratitude for the discovery.

1 lb sunchokes, scrubbed clean, unpeeled and cut into 1-inch pieces (about 2 cups)

4 Tbsp olive oil

4 leeks, whites only, sliced

2 stalks celery, diced medium

¼ cup minced garlic (10–12 cloves)

4 cups Vegetable Stock (page 250)

2 cups whipping cream

2 Tbsp fresh thyme leaves

2 tsp salt

Pepper

Serves 6–8

Preheat the oven to 400°F. Line a baking sheet with parchment paper.

Toss the sunchoke pieces in 2 Tbsp of the olive oil and place them on the prepared baking sheet. Roast for 10 minutes, then turn them over and roast for an additional 10 to 15 minutes, or until they are tender (they should be dark brown but not burned). Remove from the oven and set aside.

Heat the remaining 2 Tbsp olive oil in a large, heavy-bottomed soup pot over medium heat, and add the leeks, celery and garlic. Sauté for 20 minutes or until tender. Add the sunchoke pieces and the stock and bring to a boil. Reduce the heat and simmer uncovered for 30 minutes.

Add the cream, thyme and salt. Use an immersion blender, food processor or traditional blender to purée the soup until smooth. Season to taste with salt and pepper.

Vegan Yam and Coconut Soup

This is a killer vegan soup with a nice kick. It's quick to make, has a silky texture with a rich flavor and is deeply satisfying.

4 medium yams

¼ cup canola oil

1 medium yellow onion, diced

2 medium carrots, diced

2 stalks celery, diced

4-inch piece fresh ginger, chopped

2 Tbsp Madras curry powder

2 Tbsp sambal oelek (or
chili garlic sauce)

4 cups coconut milk

4 cups Vegetable Stock (page 250)

4 tsp lime juice (1 medium lime)

¼ cup fresh mint leaves

Serves 6

Preheat the oven to 400°F.

Pierce the yams with a fork and place them on a baking sheet. Bake until soft, about 30 minutes. Remove the yams from the oven and allow to cool, then scoop the flesh out of the skins. Discard the skins and set aside the flesh.

Heat the oil in a large, heavy-bottomed soup pot over medium heat. Add the onion, then the carrots, celery and ginger, and sauté for 10 minutes. Add the curry powder and sambal oelek, and sauté for an additional 10 minutes or until the vegetables are tender. Add the yam flesh, coconut milk and vegetable stock, and stir to combine. Bring to a boil, then reduce the heat and simmer uncovered for 1 hour.

Remove from the heat, and add the lime juice then the mint leaves. Use a hand-held immersion blender, food processor or traditional blender to blend the soup until smooth.

Surfer Noodle Soup

Tofino is a young town (the average age is 34), and a lot of the folks surf year round in weather that is unpredictable, to say the least. We first served this soup in takeout coffee cups so those who were standing in front of the truck could start sipping the broth straight away to take the chill off their bones. It wasn't uncommon for one person to pick up half a dozen cups and take them down to the beach, chopsticks in hand, to warm their friends.

2 strips kombu (dried kelp), about 4 inches × 4 inches and paper thin

2 cups bonito flakes

2 Tbsp canola oil

½ lb (about 8–10) shiitake mushrooms, de-stemmed and sliced

¼ cup soy sauce

¼ cup light miso paste

4 cups udon noodles (usually 4 standard supermarket packs)

One 12 oz package smoked tofu, diced small

1 thinly sliced green onion, green and white parts

Serves 4–6

In a large, heavy-bottomed soup pot, place 4 quarts of cold water. Add the kombu, and bring to a boil. Add the bonito flakes and turn off the heat. Let the broth steep for 20 minutes. The bonito flakes should sink to the bottom. Strain and discard the kombu and bonito flakes, leaving behind a clear liquid. Set aside.

Heat the oil in a small saucepan over a high heat, and sauté the shiitakes quickly so they do not burn, stirring frequently.

When you're ready to prepare the soup, bring the liquid to a boil again, then turn off the heat. Add the soy sauce and whisk in the miso paste. Right before serving, cook the noodles according to the package directions (there are dried versions and precooked brands, so the directions vary). Fill each serving bowl one-third full with udon noodles, and sprinkle them with diced tofu, shiitakes and green onion. Pour in hot miso broth right to the brim and serve.

. . . .

COOK'S NOTE: *Kombu, udon and bonito flakes can be found at most Japanese food markets. We are lucky enough to have a small specialty grocery store in Tofino called Beaches that carries all the ingredients for this soup, even the Soya Nova smoked tofu, produced on Salt Spring Island with non-GMO Canadian soy beans (the very same that we use in the restaurant). If you can't find smoked tofu, you can use a firm organic tofu, which is still lovely just not as smoky.*

Smoked Salmon Chowder

When we first opened the SoBo food truck, everyone and their brother in Tofino made a clam chowder—except us. At least 20 times a day we'd get a request for chowder, but I resisted until one day the request came from Artie's mother when she was visiting from New Brunswick. "Why would you not have a chowder, dear? Everyone loves a good chowder!" I reluctantly took her advice, but just to be different I used salmon rather than clams. It's still on the menu and is probably the most popular item we offer—proof that sometimes a mother does indeed know best!

6 Tbsp canola oil

3 large yellow onions, diced medium

3 large carrots, diced medium

6 stalks celery, diced medium

1 lb potatoes, cubed medium

4 cups Fish Stock (page 251)

2 Tbsp dried oregano (I use Mexican Oregano)

1 Tbsp dried basil

1 Tbsp dried thyme

1 Tbsp salt

½ cup Roasted Garlic (page 252)

1 small roasted red bell pepper (page 252)

3 cups whipping cream

1 lb smoked salmon, boneless and roughly chopped

One 7 oz can chipotle chilies in adobo sauce

1 lb fresh salmon, cut into bite-sized chunks

1 Tbsp fresh dill

Serves 6–8

Heat 4 Tbsp of the oil in a large, heavy-bottomed soup pot over medium heat and sauté about 3 cups of the onion (reserving 2 Tbsp) with the carrots and celery for 25 minutes, or until tender. Add the potatoes, stock, oregano, basil, thyme and salt and simmer uncovered for 20 minutes.

Use a food processor to purée the garlic and red pepper. Add to the soup, together with the cream and the smoked salmon.

Use a food processor to purée the chipotles. You only need 1 Tbsp for this recipe, but it makes sense to purée the entire can. Store the remainder in a sealed container in the fridge for 3 to 4 days.

Add the remaining 2 Tbsp oil to a medium-sized frying pan and heat over medium-high heat. Add the fresh salmon, the remaining 2 Tbsp onion and 1 Tbsp chipotle purée. Sauté for 4 to 5 minutes then transfer to the soup pot. Simmer for 5 minutes or until the chowder is hot throughout. Garnish each bowl with a little dill.

Caribbean Geoduck Chowder

I learned to make this chowder using conch while working as a private chef on board a yacht running the waters between Miami and the Bahamas in the 1980s. Similar versions are very common in most Floridian seafood shacks. Conches have become both very difficult to get and worrisome to source as they've been badly overfished for their souvenir value as musical horns and *objets d'art*, so this recipe has been adapted to use BC's geoduck clams. The geoduck is a very large clam native to BC's coastline and is strikingly similar to the conch in texture. (The word *geoduck* comes from the Nisqually Tribe word *gwe-duk*, which means "dig deep.")

1 whole geoduck (about 1 lb)

¼ cup canola oil

1 medium yellow onion, diced medium

2 medium carrots, diced medium

2 stalks celery, diced medium

1 green bell pepper, diced medium

2 bay leaves

4 medium red potatoes, diced medium

½ cup tomato paste

4 quarts Fish Stock (page 251)

⅔ cup day-old ½-inch bread cubes (about 1 slice bread)

½ cup Worcestershire sauce

¼ cup Louisiana-style hot sauce (I like Frank's RedHot)

1 Tbsp pepper

2 oz dry sherry

¼ cup chopped flat-leaf parsley

Serves 10

Fill a large stockpot with cold water and bring to a boil. Put the whole geoduck in the water to cook for 2 minutes then transfer it to a large bowl of ice water to halt the cooking process. This step allows the clam's shell to open so that you can easily peel off the outer trunk skin (the clam's arm).

When the geoduck is cool enough to handle, roll up the outer trunk skin until it has fully peeled off and then discard it. This exposes the white flesh of the clam. Slice the clam flesh into thick coins, about 1 inch thick, and carefully pulse them a few times in a food processor fitted with a steel blade. You want smaller pieces, not a paste. Alternatively, you can dice the pieces very small by hand. Set aside.

Heat the oil in a large, heavy-bottomed soup pot over medium heat and add the onion, then the carrots, celery, bell pepper and bay leaves, and cook until soft, 10 to 15 minutes. Add the potatoes and stir frequently with a wooden spoon for 5 minutes. Add the tomato paste and stir again for 3 minutes. Add the fish stock and bring to a boil. Reduce the heat and allow to simmer uncovered for 45 minutes.

Add the geoduck, bread cubes, Worcestershire sauce, hot sauce and pepper and stir to combine. Remove from the heat. Stir again and then allow the chowder to sit for 15 minutes before serving, so the geoduck steeps in the broth. If you'd like to keep this chowder gluten-free, omit the bread cubes and add 1 cup of cooked long-grain white or brown rice to help thicken the soup.

Drizzle sherry into each bowl of chowder before serving. Garnish with parsley.

. . . .

COOK'S NOTE: *If you don't have geoduck in your local markets or on your docks, the same weight in smaller clams can be used. Be sure to lightly steam them first until they open and then remove them from their shells. Add to the soup right before serving to ensure that they don't get overcooked.*

Black Bean Soup with *Pico de Gallo*

I first made this soup when I was the chef at Fossil Rim Wildlife Park in Glen Rose, Texas. Black beans are one of my favorite soup bases, and they make a great backdrop for a proper *pico de gallo* (it's a little spicy, but nothing too frightening). *Pico de gallo*, also known as *salsa fresca*, is Spanish for "rooster's beak." (Note: The beans in this recipe need to be soaked overnight. If you forget to soak them, or don't have time, increase the simmering time to 2 ½ hours.)

2 cups dried black beans

2 medium green bell peppers, diced medium

2 whole cloves garlic plus 4 cloves garlic, minced

1 large white onion, diced small

3 bay leaves

3 Tbsp olive oil

2 stalks celery, diced small

1 carrot, diced small

½ cup dry white wine

4 cups Vegetable Stock (page 250)

2 Tbsp salt

1 tsp white vinegar

1 tsp ground cumin

1 tsp dried oregano

¼ cup sour cream

Pico de Gallo (see below)

Serves 4

To prepare the beans, rinse them thoroughly in a strainer under cold running water then transfer to a large, heavy-bottomed soup pot containing 8 cups of cold water. Let the beans soak overnight in the fridge.

Drain the beans and return them to the pot with another 8 cups of fresh cold water. Add ½ cup of the bell peppers, 2 whole cloves of garlic, half the onion and 1 bay leaf and bring to a boil. Reduce the heat, loosely cover and simmer for about 1 ½ hours until the beans are tender, stirring occasionally. Remove from the heat and set aside.

Heat the oil in a medium-sized frying pan over medium heat, and add the remaining bell pepper, garlic and onion with the celery and carrot. Cook for 4 to 5 minutes. Add the wine and cook, uncovered, until it has evaporated, 2 to 3 minutes.

Transfer the sautéed vegetables to the pot containing the beans. Add the vegetable stock, salt, vinegar, cumin, oregano and remaining bay leaves. Simmer covered for 10 to 15 minutes.

Remove the bay leaves. Use a slotted spoon to transfer 2 cups of the beans to a bowl. Mash the beans with the back of a wooden spoon or a pestle then stir them back into the soup to give it a creamy consistency.

Ladle the soup into bowls and garnish each with a dollop of sour cream and a few spoonfuls of *pico de gallo*.

Pico de Gallo

4 plum tomatoes, seeded, diced small

2 serrano chilies, seeded, diced small

1 white onion, diced small

½ cup chopped fresh cilantro

2 Tbsp lime juice (1 medium lime)

2 tsp salt

Combine all the ingredients in a bowl. Let them sit for about 10 minutes to let the flavors marry.

Makes 1 cup

Aztec Bean Soup

I just love heritage beans, and for this recipe I use Painted Ponies, Tiger Eyes and Octobers. They have creamier textures, seem much sturdier and don't mush as quickly as the ones typically found in big-box supermarkets. This soup is best in the early fall when the squash has just been picked and the last of the fresh corn is being harvested.

1 cup dried heritage beans (if you can't find these, use dried black beans)

2 bay leaves

2 Tbsp salt

1 Tbsp cumin seeds

1 Tbsp coriander seeds

1 Tbsp chili powder

¼ cup canola oil

2 white onions, diced small

2 carrots, diced small

2 stalks celery, diced small

2 Tbsp minced garlic (6–8 cloves)

1 sweet potato, peeled, diced small

2 cups canned or fresh tomatoes, crushed (2–3 medium tomatoes)

½ cup roasted green chilies, diced small (canned or see page 252)

8 cups Vegetable Stock (page 250)

1 cup corn kernels (fresh or frozen and thawed)

Serves 6, with some left over for freezing

Wash the beans well in a colander, then transfer them to a large, heavy-bottomed soup pot. Add 4 cups of water and the bay leaves. Bring to a boil, cover, turn the heat to low and simmer for 1 ½ hours or until the beans are tender. Add the salt and then drain the beans. Set aside.

In a small frying pan over medium heat, toast the cumin seeds, coriander seeds and chili powder for 5 minutes, tossing constantly to avoid burning. Remove from the heat and grind them together in a spice grinder or with a mortar and pestle.

Heat the oil in a large, heavy-bottomed soup pot over medium heat and add the onions, carrots, celery and garlic. Sauté for 15 minutes or until the vegetables are soft. Add the ground spices and sweet potato and sauté for 10 more minutes.

Add the tomatoes and green chilies then the stock. Turn the heat to low and simmer uncovered for 30 minutes. Add the corn and beans, and simmer for another 10 minutes.

Salt to taste and serve.

. . . .

COOK'S NOTE: *Green chilies can be found in the can in most supermarkets. I prefer to roast my own poblanos or Anaheims for this recipe, but canned is a quicker option.*

Heritage Squash and Poblano Soup

Whether it's buttercup, butternut, kabocha, sweet dumpling, turban or the humble pumpkin, any and all squash will work for this soup. Follow the same roasting methods and adjust the roasting times according to the size of the squash.

2–3 lb squash

4 Tbsp olive oil

1 or 2 poblano chilies
(2 if you like it hot)

4 Tbsp butter

3 apples, peeled, cored and
sliced (preferably Granny Smith,
Fuji, Pippin or Pink Lady)

2 large leeks, whites only, sliced

1 medium carrot, diced small

2 stalks celery, diced small

6 cups Vegetable Stock (page 250)

1 tsp salt

2 cups whipping cream

1 Tbsp fresh thyme leaves

Serves 6–8

Preheat the oven to 400°F. Line a baking sheet with parchment paper.

Cut the squash in half and scoop out the seeds (save them for roasting later). Rub 1 Tbsp of the olive oil on the flesh of the squash, and prick the outer skin with a fork. Lay the squash cut side down on the prepared baking sheet and bake for 30 to 40 minutes, or until the squash flesh is tender and easy to scoop out. After 25 minutes add 1 cup of water or vegetable stock to the pan to keep it from browning and allow the squash to steam for the last 5 minutes of cooking.

Remove the squash from the oven (keep the oven on) and allow to cool, about 30 minutes. Scoop the flesh out with a firm spoon and set aside. Discard the skin.

Meanwhile place the poblano chilies on a baking sheet and bake for 20 minutes or until they are dark all over. Remove from the oven (keep the oven on) and place in a bowl, covered, for 20 minutes. This will help to steam off the skin. When they are cool enough to handle, remove the stems and skins and set the chilies aside.

Heat the remaining 3 Tbsp olive oil in a large, heavy-bottomed soup pot over medium heat and add the butter, apples, leek, carrot and celery. Sauté for 20 minutes, until tender. Add the poblanos and cooked squash with the stock and salt. Turn the heat to low and simmer uncovered for 30 minutes.

Meanwhile clean the squash seeds of any stringy flesh then wash them. Pat them dry and place them, on a parchment-lined baking sheet, in the oven for 10 to 15 minutes.

Add the cream and thyme leaves to the soup. Purée the soup using an immersion blender, food processor or traditional blender until smooth and silky. Use the toasted seeds as a garnish.

Blending Soup

If you are using a traditional blender, please be careful if you are blending the soup while it's hot. Pulse it at first and keep the lid on with your hand wrapped in a dish towel or cloth. I have seen many a professional chef get a face full of scalding hot soup by cutting this corner.

French Green Lentil and Roasted Shiitake Soup

This is an earthy bowl of comfort soup that gets better with age (I'd recommend refrigerating it and eating on day 3, and definitely by day 5). The little drizzle of balsamic vinegar at the end really makes it sing.

4 cups French green or puy lentils
(regular brown lentils are fine as well)

4 quarts Vegetable Stock (page 250)

½ lb (about 10) fresh
shiitake mushrooms, de-
stemmed, thinly sliced

¼ cup plus 2 Tbsp olive oil

2 large yellow onions, diced small

2 medium carrots, diced small

4 stalks celery, diced small

¼ cup roughly chopped
garlic (10–12 cloves)

½ lb red potatoes, diced small

2 cups roughly chopped tomatoes
(2–3 medium tomatoes)

1 bay leaf

2 Tbsp chopped fresh thyme leaves

1 Tbsp salt

2 Tbsp sherry vinegar

2 Tbsp balsamic vinegar

Serves 10

Wash the lentils in a colander until the water runs clear. Transfer them to a large, heavy-bottomed soup pot and add the stock. Simmer the lentils uncovered for 1 hour. Skim off any foam that rises to the surface. After 1 hour, the lentils should be soft and tender but still intact. If you boil them too quickly, they will break apart and get mushy. Set them aside, leaving them in the soup pot.

Preheat the oven to 400°F.

Coat the mushrooms with the 2 Tbsp oil and place them on a baking sheet. Roast the mushrooms for 10 minutes. Remove from the oven and set aside.

Heat the remaining ¼ cup oil in a large saucepan over medium heat, and sauté the onion, carrot and celery until tender, about 15 minutes. Add the garlic then the potatoes, and sauté for another 10 minutes. Add the tomatoes, bay leaf, thyme and salt, and stir to combine.

Transfer the vegetables to the pot with the lentils and simmer uncovered over low heat for another 30 minutes. Turn off the heat, and stir in the mushrooms and sherry vinegar.

Serve with a drizzle of balsamic vinegar.

Health in a Bowl

When my dad was battling cancer his throat was often so sore after his radiation treatments that he couldn't eat. To ensure he was getting the nutrition he needed, I made this soup and puréed it until it was silky smooth. He called it "health in a bowl," and it actually tasted better puréed. It's something I rarely make these days, but it's just so delicious and it takes me back to the last precious months that I got to spend loving and looking after my dad.

1 ½ cups dried red lentils

4 cups Vegetable Stock (page 250)

2 Tbsp olive oil

4 large leeks, whites only, sliced

2 Tbsp Madras curry powder (a little hotter than most)

5 medium carrots, grated

2 medium zucchini, diced small

2 Tbsp salt

Cilantro Cream (see below)

1 cup plain yogurt

Serves 8

Wash the lentils in a colander until the water runs clear. Transfer them to a large, heavy-bottomed soup pot and add the stock. Bring to a boil, then turn down the heat and simmer uncovered for 15 minutes.

Meanwhile, heat the olive oil in a medium-sized frying pan over medium-high heat, and sauté the leeks with the curry powder for 10 to 15 minutes, or until tender. Transfer them to the soup pot and add the carrots, zucchini and salt. Cook uncovered over medium heat for 20 minutes, or until tender. You may need to add more stock or some water. You want about 2 inches of liquid above the vegetables. While the soup is simmering, prepare the cilantro cream.

Add the yogurt to the soup and use an immersion blender, food processor or traditional blender to blend it until it is a smooth purée.

Season with salt to taste, and garnish each bowl with 1 Tbsp cilantro cream.

· ·

COOK'S NOTE: *This soup can be served as a main course as it is very hearty, healthy and super-low in fat.*

Cilantro Cream

½ cup plain yogurt

¼ cup chopped fresh cilantro

2 tsp chopped fresh mint

Pinch salt

Makes ½ cup

Blend all the ingredients together for 1 minute in a blender or whisk by hand to combine. Refrigerate for up to 4 days or freeze for up to 6 months.

Roasted Winter Vegetable Soup

Tofino gets around 11 feet of rain on average per year, so we need to know how to stay nourished and healthy. This soup is packed with creamy cannellini beans, tomato, garlic and harvest-fresh vegetables, not to mention it's high in vitamin D, zinc and magnesium.

¼ cup olive oil

2 leeks, whites only, sliced

2 medium carrots, diced medium

2 stalks celery, diced medium

5 large cloves garlic, minced

2 Yukon Gold potatoes, skin on, diced medium

1 large roasted red bell pepper, puréed (page 252)

2 Tbsp salt

1 tsp saffron

2 Tbsp canola oil

½ lb (8–10) shiitake mushrooms, de-stemmed and sliced

3 quarts Vegetable Stock (page 250)

2 cups roughly chopped tomatoes (2–3 medium tomatoes)

1 cup dried cannellini beans, soaked and cooked (see method page 213)

Cilantro Pesto (see below)

Serves 4–6

Place the olive oil in a large, heavy-bottomed soup pot over medium heat. Add the leeks, carrots and celery and sauté together until tender. Add the garlic then the potatoes, red peppers, salt and saffron, and sauté for an additional 15 minutes. Heat the canola oil in a small saucepan over a high heat, and sauté the shiitakes quickly so they do not burn, stirring frequently. Add the stock, tomatoes, shiitakes and beans to the stock pot and simmer uncovered for 20 minutes. While the soup is simmering prepare the cilantro pesto.

Serve the soup in bowls and swirl in a little cilantro pesto as garnish.

Cilantro Pesto

2 bunches cilantro

½ cup pumpkin seeds

¼ cup grated Parmesan cheese

2 Tbsp minced garlic (6–8 cloves)

½ tsp chili flakes

½ tsp salt

¼ cup olive oil

Combine all the ingredients except the oil in a food processor. While the processor is running, pour in the oil slowly until the dressing has emulsified. Refrigerate for up to 1 week, or freeze for up to 6 months.

Makes 1 cup

Salads

Dungeness Crab and Fennel Salad 86

Grilled Watermelon and Shrimp Salad 88

Albacore Tuna Salad 90

Roasted Squash Salad with Goat Cheese and Toasted Hazelnuts 92

Wild Rice and Dried Berry Salad 94

Italian Spring Salad 95

Botanical Garden Salad 97

Heirloom Tomato Salad 98

Pacific Rim Salad with Ginger and Soy 101

Seaweed Salad 102

Dungeness Crab and Fennel Salad

It makes me feel like the luckiest chef on earth to look out my window early in the morning and see our veteran crab fisherman, Peter White, pulling up his traps from the water and rocking out to the radio. His hard work inspires me to create dishes that would make him proud. This is one of them.

Citrus Vinaigrette (page 87)

¼ cup pumpkin seeds

1 lb fresh cooked hard-shell crabmeat (Dungeness, if available, not soft-shell or canned)

2 ruby red or pink grapefruits, sectioned (see sidebar below)

1 bulb fennel, white only, cored and very thinly shaved

1 cup mizuna or arugula leaves

1 avocado, thinly sliced

Serves 4, for a light lunch or appetizer

Preheat the oven to 400°F.

Prepare the citrus vinaigrette. While it is reducing, spread the pumpkin seeds on a baking sheet and toast in the oven for 5 minutes. Remove from the oven and set aside.

In a large bowl, gently mix together the crab, grapefruit sections and fennel. Add the greens and the dressing. Add the avocado at the end to minimize browning and so the slices don't break up. Garnish with the toasted pumpkin seeds.

. . . .

COOK'S NOTE: *Hard-shelled crab such as Dungeness is our local Pacific Coast crab of choice, but you should use the crab that is freshest in your region. I would suggest Lump Blue crab from the East Coast. King and queen crabs are also beautiful. (You may know queen crab by its other name, snow crab.)*

Prepping Grapefruit

Wash the grapefruit thoroughly. Peel it by first cutting slices off both the top and bottom. This prevents the fruit from rolling and allows you to get a steady grip on a level cutting surface. Run your knife along the peel from top to bottom, removing the skin and pith. To section the grapefruit, hold the fruit in your hand and run a paring knife along each side of the membrane walls between sections until it gets to the center core. Do this over a bowl to catch the juice. It's tricky, but once you become used to the back and forth movement of it, you'll find it's no longer a chore.

Citrus Vinaigrette

1 cup orange juice

½ cup apple juice

2 Tbsp lime juice (1 medium lime)

1 large shallot, minced

1 ½ Tbsp red wine vinegar

1 Tbsp sambal oelek (or
chili garlic sauce)

1 tsp salt

¼ cup olive oil

Makes 1 cup

Heat the orange juice in a medium-sized saucepan over low heat. You are aiming to reduce it by half, about 10 minutes. Add the apple juice, lime juice, shallots, vinegar, chili sauce and salt, then add the oil slowly, whisking until the dressing has emulsified. Refrigerate for up to 1 week.

Grilled Watermelon and Shrimp Salad

I first came up with this recipe when I was cooking in Florida. Sturdy, sweet and succulent rock shrimp were abundant on the docks and watermelon was at every roadside produce stand. This is the version that I make today at SoBo. The local humpback shrimp are a great stand-in for rock shrimp, and I just love grilling watermelon. It adds a wonderful depth of flavor and an irresistible smokiness.

1 small watermelon, cut into 1-inch-thick wheels, skin removed

¼ cup olive oil, plus extra to prep for grilling

1 cucumber, sliced into thick coins and kept cold

½ cup chopped fresh mint leaves

¼ cup lime juice (2 medium limes)

2 tsp salt

12–20 large shrimp or prawns, peeled and deveined

¼ cup pumpkin seeds, toasted

Serves 4

Preheat the BBQ to high. You should not be able to hold your hand over it for more than a few seconds.

Brush the watermelon lightly with a little olive oil to prevent sticking. Lay the slices directly on the grill racks and grill for 2 to 3 minutes. When they start to loosen and can easily be lifted from the grill, turn them over and grill on the other side for another 2 to 3 minutes, or until nicely charred. Lightly salt them then remove from the grill and dice into medium-sized chunks.

In a large bowl, gently toss the still warm watermelon with the cold cucumber, mint, lime juice and salt and the ¼ cup olive oil.

Lightly brush the shrimp with more olive oil and grill for 30 seconds per side or until they begin to turn pink or red. Divide the salad between four plates and top with the hot shrimp, then sprinkle with pumpkin seeds.

Albacore Tuna Salad

Sashimi-grade tuna is a must for this recipe. I use the albacore fished off our coast. It's creamier and less sinewy than other species. Don't use frozen corn kernels for this recipe. For salads I think you should go fresh or go without.

½ cup extra virgin olive oil

2 tsp salt

1 lb albacore tuna loin (sashimi grade) cut into 4 equal portions

4 cups mixed greens

2 tomatoes, cut into wedges

1 cucumber, sliced into coins

8 chives

1 cup Fire-Roasted Corn (page 217)

1 tsp pepper (optional but I really like it on my greens)

2 Tbsp balsamic vinegar

Serves 4

See photo on page 84

Heat half the oil in a large, heavy-bottomed frying pan over high heat. Salt the tuna and lay it carefully in the frying pan. There are three sides to each loin, so cook for 1 to 2 minutes per side. When done, the tuna will be golden on the outside and medium-rare inside. Remove the tuna from the pan, and allow to rest while tossing the salad.

Arrange the greens, tomatoes, cucumber slices and chives on each plate. Scatter the corn kernels overtop. Season to taste with the pepper. Thinly slice each portion of tuna and fan out overtop the salad. Mix the remaining ¼ cup oil with the vinegar and serve on the side as an optional condiment.

. . . .

COOK'S NOTE: *If you've been wondering what to do with the premium extra virgin olive oil languishing in your pantry, this is the perfect way to use it! With so few ingredients in this recipe, it's important to use only the best.*

Ian Bryce
NANOOSE BAY, BC

Ian Bryce was always a provider, even as a kid. "Fish, game, wild forage foods, you name it," he says. "It's always been important to me to feed people and to feed them well. All of my family were avid sports-fishermen, so fresh salmon was a summer staple when I wasgrowing up. Barbecued salmon burgers at my grandparents' place were my favorite—a fresh bun, some mayonnaise, a little salt and pepper and a slab of warm fresh coho. I've always taken deep satisfaction from knowing my fish is well served to people who appreciate it."

After starting his adult life as a lawyer, Ian went back to his roots to skipper his family's fishing boat, the *NERKA #1*. Based out of Nanoose Bay, he's now our most trusted source for albacore tuna, caught in offshore waters between California and Haida Gwaii.

The albacore fishery is one of the greenest and cleanest in the world, and Ian's fish have been recognized by the Marine Stewardship Council, the Vancouver Aquarium's Ocean Wise program and the Monterey Bay Aquarium's Seafood Watch program. Ian does it all himself—lands the fish, calls for the order, delivers to my door and picks up his check. That's the way I like to do business.

Roasted Squash Salad
with Goat Cheese and Toasted Hazelnuts

This is an earthy salad that makes for a very satisfying lunch or light dinner and with toasted hazelnuts you just can't go wrong. In a pinch, blue cheese and walnuts can be substituted for goat's cheese and hazelnuts.

2 lb butternut squash
(1 medium squash)

2 Tbsp canola oil

1 cup whole hazelnuts

Port Wine Vinaigrette (see below)

2 tsp salt

4 cups mixed greens

1 cup crumbled goat cheese

Pepper

Serves 4

Preheat the oven to 400°F.

Peel the squash and dice it into ¾-inch cubes. Toss the cubes in the oil, place them on a baking sheet and roast for 20 to 25 minutes, until soft. Remove from the oven and let cool to room temperature.

Arrange the hazelnuts on a baking sheet and bake for 5 minutes. Remove from the oven, let cool for about 3 minutes then place them on a clean kitchen towel and give them a good rub to remove the skins. While they are baking or cooling, prepare the port wine vinaigrette.

In a large bowl, season the squash with the salt then toss with the toasted hazelnuts, greens, goat cheese and vinaigrette. Season with pepper to taste.

Port Wine Vinaigrette

⅓ cup apple cider vinegar

¼ cup port

3 Tbsp orange juice

1 ½ Tbsp pure maple syrup

1 tsp brown sugar

1 tsp minced shallots
(about ⅓ shallot)

½ tsp salt

½ cup olive oil

Makes 1 cup

Combine all the ingredients, except the oil, in a small bowl. Add the oil slowly, whisking until the dressing has emulsified. Refrigerate for up to 1 week.

Wild Rice and Dried Berry Salad

I like the contrasting flavors and textures of this salad. The pecans are crunchy, the fruit is chewy and the rice has a texture somewhere in between. The herbaceous flavor of the wild rice is complemented really nicely by the sweet tartness of the cranberries and cherries. It's a beautifully balanced dish that tastes great hot or cold, and lends itself well to game birds, like quail, or served on its own over a bed of baby field greens.

1 cup uncooked wild rice

4–5 cups Vegetable Stock (page 250) or water

¼ tsp salt

¼ cup pecan halves

¼ cup dried cranberries

¼ cup dried cherries

3 green onions, thinly sliced

¼ cup mix of cranberry and orange juice

1 Tbsp orange zest

Salt

Serves 4, as a side salad

Rinse the rice under cold water until the water runs clear. Place the rice, stock and salt in a heavy-bottomed saucepan. Bring to a boil and then reduce the heat to a simmer. Cover and cook for about 45 minutes or until the rice is tender, adding more stock if necessary.

Preheat the oven to 400°F.

While the rice is cooking, toast the pecans on a baking sheet in the oven for about 5 minutes.

When the rice is cooked, rinse it again to cool and then drain.

Mix the rice with the pecans, dried fruit, green onions, fruit juice and orange zest. Season to taste with salt.

Italian Spring Salad

After a long, cold winter, our taste buds and bodies both need a wake-up call. This salad hits the mark with fresh pea tendrils and young arugula. Their youth is key, as arugula and pea tendrils get tough and bitter as the season matures. Pea tendrils are simply the shoots before the sugar snap peas or shelling peas blossom. They are grassy and sweet and make a wonderful contrast to the sharper arugula. Sections of blood orange are an attractive and sweet option for this salad. It can also be ramped up with sautéed scallops or prawns. Remember that a recipe is a starting point. I encourage home cooks to play around!

Champagne Vinaigrette (see below)

2 cups arugula

2 cups pea tendrils

8 slices prosciutto or any dried cured ham

½ cup shaved Parmesan cheese

Serves 4, as a side salad

Prepare the champagne vinaigrette.

Combine the arugula and pea tendrils in a large bowl, and lightly toss in the vinaigrette. Arrange the prosciutto and Parmesan on top.

Champagne Vinaigrette

½ cup champagne vinegar

2 Tbsp red wine vinegar

2 medium shallots, minced

1 Tbsp minced garlic (3–4 cloves)

1 tsp salt

1 tsp Dijon mustard

1 tsp honey

½ cup olive oil

Makes 1 cup

Combine both vinegars with the shallots, garlic and salt in a large bowl. Let them sit for 20 minutes to marinate. Add the mustard and honey, then add the oil slowly, whisking until the dressing has emulsified. Store in the fridge for up to 1 week.

. . . .

COOK'S NOTE: *The magic ratio for vinaigrette is usually 3 parts oil to 1 part vinegar. However, you will notice that most of my vinaigrettes are more like 2:1 or in this case almost 1:1. I simply find most vinaigrettes are too oily and I very much enjoy the flavor of vinegars. Feel free to add more oil if that's what you prefer.*

Barbara and Lorne Ebell
NANOOSE BAY, BC

Barbara (pictured) and Lorne Ebell of Nanoose Edibles Organic Farm tend a small farm on the fertile east side of Vancouver Island, and have been supplying SoBo with organic greens and vegetables for well over a decade. They started farming 20 years ago as a retirement venture and now, in their mid-80s, they're showing few signs of slowing down.

Barbara's love of good food started early in life when, as a young girl, she would visit her Swedish family at Christmastime. "I remember going with my aunt to the sod house where their winter vegetables were stored," she says. "She'd put them on the cutting board in the kitchen and cut them into slices, and my cousins and I would eat them just like that."

Nanoose Edibles was certified organic in 1997 and now, besides the quiet daily work of planting, picking and preparing produce for market, the Ebells spend much of their time passing on their knowledge to students and visitors to the farm. I asked Barbara once why she does what she does, and she simply replied, "What else would I be doing? Playing bridge or being stuck inside? I'm outdoors most of the time working with students. They keep me young, they keep me up to date and they keep reminding me why we do it—to do our part in building a healthy planet." Having lived without the convenience of supermarkets, Barbara has never forgotten the health and community benefits of locally grown food. The people of Vancouver Island are blessed to have folks like the Ebells stewarding the land.

Botanical Garden Salad

This is just the thing when you need a really refreshing and healthy salad without any bells and whistles beyond a good kick of acidity. The key here is to use the very finest olive oil and vinegar available to you, and, of course, the freshest salad greens!

1 cup Balsamic Vinaigrette (see below)

¼ cup pumpkin seeds

4 cups mixed greens

2 cups spinach or baby spinach

1 small raw beet, julienned

⅓ long cucumber, julienned

1 medium carrot, julienned

½ medium red bell pepper, julienned

1 tomato, cut into 8 wedges

Serves 4

Preheat the oven to 400°F.

Prepare the balsamic vinaigrette. While it is marinating, place the pumpkin seeds on a baking sheet and toast in the oven for 5 minutes. Remove from the oven and set aside.

Toss the greens, spinach, beet, cucumber, carrot, bell pepper and tomato together in a large bowl. Add the vinaigrette and toss lightly until well coated. Garnish with the toasted pumpkin seeds.

Balsamic Vinaigrette

¼ cup sherry vinegar

¼ cup balsamic vinegar

2 medium shallots

1 tsp salt

2 Tbsp minced garlic (6–8 cloves)

2 Tbsp puréed Roasted Garlic (page 252)

1 Tbsp Dijon mustard

1 tsp sugar

1 tsp fresh thyme leaves

1 tsp chopped flat-leaf parsley

1 cup olive oil

Makes 1 ½ cups

Combine both vinegars in a blender, and add the shallots and salt. Let them sit to marinate for 20 minutes. Add both garlics, the mustard, sugar and herbs to the blender. Pulse as you slowly drizzle in the oil until the dressing has emulsified. This will keep in an airtight container in the fridge for 1 week.

COOK'S NOTE: *This simple yet versatile vinaigrette is also excellent on a pasta salad. Just add grilled veggies and fusilli or farfalle, and top with fresh basil and Parmesan.*

Heirloom Tomato Salad

I love tomatoes when they're fresh and ripe—they can be of almost any variety as long as they're in season and at their best. I live on them when they're in the garden and I preserve them like crazy so I can have them all year round. To be honest, though, I usually run out by early November!

Sherry Balsamic Vinaigrette
(see below)

2 large heirloom tomatoes,
each cut into 16 wedges

½ tsp salt plus more to taste

4 cups mixed greens

1 cup hand-torn fresh basil leaves

Serves 4, as a side salad

Prepare the sherry balsamic vinaigrette.

Add the tomatoes to a large bowl and season to taste with salt. Add the greens, basil and ½ tsp salt and toss with the sherry balsamic vinaigrette.

. . . .

COOK'S NOTE: *If you use heirloom tomatoes of different varieties and sizes, this very simple salad makes a strong visual impact.*

Sherry Balsamic Vinaigrette

2 Tbsp sherry vinegar

2 Tbsp red wine vinegar

2 Tbsp balsamic vinegar

2 medium shallots, minced

2 Tbsp chopped flat-leaf parsley

2 Tbsp puréed Roasted
Garlic (page 252)

1 Tbsp minced garlic (3–4 cloves)

1 cup olive oil

Makes 1 ½ cups

Combine all the ingredients, except the oil, in a large bowl, and let them sit for 20 minutes to marinate. Add the oil slowly, whisking until the dressing has emulsified. Refrigerate for up to 1 week.

Pacific Rim Salad
with Ginger and Soy

If I could only eat one dressing for the rest of my life, it would be my Ginger Soy Vinaigrette. The zesty, punchy combo of soy and ginger has always pounced on my palate, especially with raw veggies and lettuces. This salad is a wonderful base for a grilled piece of fish, chicken or even tofu.

Ginger Soy Vinaigrette (see below)

2 cups fresh lettuce mix (try to source an Asian greens mix)

½ medium beet, peeled and julienned

½ small jicama, peeled and julienned

¼ medium red bell pepper, julienned

1 medium carrot, julienned

10 snow peas, string removed and julienned

½ cup sunflower sprouts

2 Tbsp toasted sesame seeds

Serves 4, as a side salad

Prepare the ginger soy vinaigrette.

Build the salad by stacking the ingredients on top of each other, in the order listed. Drizzle the vinaigrette over top.

Ginger Soy Vinaigrette

¼ cup soy sauce

2 Tbsp mirin

2-inch piece fresh ginger, minced

1 green onion, chopped

2 Tbsp mushroom soy sauce

1 Tbsp rice vinegar

1 Tbsp lime juice (1 small lime)

1 Tbsp minced garlic (3–4 cloves)

1 Tbsp honey

½ cup canola oil

1 Tbsp sesame oil

Makes 1 cup

Combine all the ingredients, expect the oils, in a large bowl. Mix well with a whisk for 30 seconds, then add the oils slowly, whisking until the dressing has emulsified. Refrigerate for up to 1 week.

. . . .

COOK'S NOTE: *This dressing is fresh, light and incredibly versatile. If you omit the oils, it's a marinade for chicken satay; if you add ½ cup tahini, it becomes a richer, creamier dressing suitable for a seaweed salad or as a sauce with noodles.*

Seaweed Salad

I fell in love with seaweed soon after moving to Tofino. A young woman named Diane Bernard walked into my kitchen one day with a bucket of seaweed straight from the shore. It smelled like a wave had just rolled into my kitchen! Though I had no experience with it, I peered into the bucket and didn't hesitate. "Sure, I'll give it a go!" Today, Diane has a thriving company called Outer Coast Seaweed. It supplies restaurants and spas all over British Columbia with seaweed and spa products.

Tahini Dressing (page 103)

6 Tbsp salt

1 cup fresh Egregia seaweed
(also known as feather boa)

1 cup fresh Alaria seaweed (also
known as winged kelp)

1 carrot, julienned

1 small cucumber, julienned

1 red bell pepper, julienned

2 Tbsp black sesame seeds

Serves 6, as a side salad

Prepare the tahini dressing.

Fill a large, heavy-bottomed soup pot with water, add the salt and bring to a boil. Rinse both seaweeds well in a colander, then transfer to the pot and blanch for 2 to 3 minutes. Remove the seaweed, drain in the colander and rinse well with cold water.

De-rib the seaweed by running a knife down either side of the thick spine to remove it (you can also use scissors). Then cut the de-ribbed Alaria into matchstick-thin strips. The de-ribbed Egregia is fine as is.

In a large bowl, toss the seaweed, carrot, cucumber and red pepper with the dressing. Sprinkle with black sesame seeds and serve.

> ### Sourcing Seaweed
>
> Fresh seaweed (like that shown in the photo opposite) is often a locally foraged product. If you're lucky enough to live near an ocean, check for local foragers who can hook you up with fresh seaweed. If fresh is not available, you can use dried hijiki, wakame or arame (available at most Asian grocery stores) instead. Just rehydrate it before using by soaking in water for 10 minutes, and drain before using. You may also be able to find already rehydrated seaweed (where the seaweed is sold packaged and moist). If you use this, make sure you follow the first step of the recipe and rinse the seaweed thoroughly to remove excess salt, then drain to remove excess water.

Tahini Dressing

¼ cup tahini paste

¼ cup soy sauce

1 medium shallot, diced

2 Tbsp red wine vinegar

1 Tbsp lime juice (1 medium lime)

1 Tbsp molasses

1 Tbsp sambal oelek (or
chili garlic sauce)

½-inch piece fresh ginger, minced

½ tsp brown sugar

½ cup canola oil

Makes 1 cup

Combine all the ingredients, except the oil, in a blender. Purée, adding the oil slowly until the dressing has emulsified. You can store this dressing in an airtight container in the fridge for up to 1 week.

Sandwiches, Burgers & Our Famous Tacos

Killer Fish Tacos with Fresh Fruit Salsa 107

Street-Style Veggie Tacos 108

Pinto Bean Burrito 111

Crispy Snapper Sandwich 112

Seafood Salad Pita Pockets 113

BBQ Brisket Sandwich 117

Grilled Veggie Sandwich 119

The Great Big Vegan Burger 120

Killer Fish Tacos
with Fresh Fruit Salsa

I've always adjusted this recipe according to what fish is readily available. In New York I used snapper, and in Texas I used bass. Here in BC, salmon and halibut have become my all-time favorites. This recipe was featured in *The Best American Recipes 2000,* edited by Fran McCullough and Suzanne Hamlin, and in *The Gourmet Cookbook*, edited by Ruth Reichl.

Fresh Fruit Salsa (see below)

1 lb wild salmon, boneless and skinless

1 lb halibut, boneless and skinless

1 Tbsp salt

½ cup olive oil

1 cup small-diced red onion (about 1 onion)

½ cup puréed canned chipotle chilies in adobo sauce

16 crispy hard taco shells

Serves 8

Prepare the fresh fruit salsa.

Cut the salmon and halibut into 1-inch cubes and season with the salt.

Heat the oil in a large frying pan over medium-high heat. Add the onion and sauté for 1 minute. Add the fish and fry for about 3 minutes, until just cooked. Add the chipotle chilies and sauté for 2 to 3 more minutes. Remove from the heat.

Fill the taco shells halfway with the fish mixture, then top with the salsa. Serve immediately, two tacos per person.

Fresh Fruit Salsa

This salsa should reflect the season, so don't be a slave to the recipe. I mix it up all the time, combining fruits like peaches and blueberries with watermelon, or pineapple with avocado—buy what's fresh!

4 kiwi fruits, diced small

½ pineapple, diced small

1 mango, diced small

1 small papaya, diced small

2 avocados, diced small

½ cup chopped fresh cilantro

Makes 5–6 cups

Combine all the ingredients and refrigerate until ready to use. This salsa will stand up for about 24 hours, after which time the fruit begins to break down.

. . . .

COOK'S NOTE: *The fruit in this salsa should be diced smaller than for a fruit salad, but not so small that the fruit turns to mush. It should amount to 5–6 cups all together. If you intend to prepare the salsa in advance, don't add the avocado until immediately before serving as avocado turns brown quickly.*

Street-Style Veggie Tacos

"Greasy little veggie tacos" is what we call this dish around our house. The key is to do them in a pan on a stove, and they need to be served at the half-crispy, half-soft stage. The pickled peppers have to touch the veggie ground round to get the unique flavor that you're looking for. That's just the way it is and I should know because I have eaten hundreds and served thousands.

Eight 6-inch soft corn tortillas

One 12 oz package Yves Veggie Ground Round (this is the only one I'd recommend)

1 cup grated Oaxaca cheese

½ cup canola oil

½ cup Pickled Jalapeños (page 255)

2 cups mixed greens

1 avocado, sliced into 8

Serves 4

Lay the tortillas on a cutting board. Place 2 Tbsp ground round on one side of each tortilla, top with 1 Tbsp cheese and fold over into a half-moon shape.

Heat 2 Tbsp of the canola oil in a cast iron frying pan over medium heat. Gently place two folded tacos in the frying pan at a time. Weigh the tacos down by placing something like a metal pie pan on top of them. The idea is to have a tight fold, not a wide-open taco. The crisping method only takes 1 or 2 minutes, so be prepared to turn the tacos as soon as the first side is crispy. The outside of the taco can burn before the insides heat up so keep a close eye on the heat.

When the tacos are crispy on each side, remove them from the frying pan and place them on paper towel to soak up any excess oil. Gently pry open each taco and fill with 1 tsp pickled jalapeños, ¼ cup mixed greens and 1 slice avocado.

· ·

COOK'S NOTE: *Oaxaca cheese is semi-soft and resembles an un-aged Monterey Jack. You can substitute cheddar or Monterey Jack as both melt well.*

Pinto Bean Burrito

Burritos are so easy to eat, making them especially handy if you're on the run. This one has been the number-one seller on the SoBo children's menu for years, and they're super kid-friendly to make at home, too. I feel really good about feeding them to the local kids because they're so healthy. Little brother and sister Mila and Jet, who live out on Beck Island, are two of this burrito's biggest fans. Their loyalty is only bested by that of famous Tofitian photographer and big kid Wayne Barnes, who has one every day of the year that SoBo is open. He adds pickled jalapeños to his order, and we call it a Waynarito. (Note that the pinto beans take 2 hours to prepare.)

2 cups Pinto Beans (page 213)

Four 10-inch whole wheat flour tortillas

1 avocado, either sliced into 12 or mashed

1 cup shredded iceberg lettuce

½ cup shredded white cheddar cheese

1 cup Roasted Tomato Salsa (page 49)

Serves 4

Heat the cooked pinto beans in a medium-sized saucepan over low heat, and keep the heat on low to keep them warm while you prepare everything else.

Preheat a large frying pan to the smoking point. Quickly heat the tortillas on both sides until pliable, about 20 seconds. Be careful not to scorch them, as it makes them brittle. Stack them on a plate once done to keep warm. If you have to hold the burritos for any length of time before serving them, wrap them in aluminum foil to keep in the heat.

Construct the burritos by layering the avocado, lettuce, cheese, salsa and warm beans in the center of each tortilla. Fold each tortilla in half with the loose edges pointing away from you. Tuck in the ends and then roll the tortilla away from you until the burrito is completely rolled.

Crispy Snapper Sandwich

The best fish sandwich I've ever had was at a busy little spot in Lake Worth, Florida, called John G's. It was the early 1980s and I remember the line was out the door every day for sweet and flaky white fish on soft kaiser rolls. The fish was so moist it would drip down my face. I came up with this recipe to honor the memory of that sandwich.

½ cup Red Pepper Aioli (page 165)

1 cup rice flour

1 cup corn flour

2 tsp salt

1 tsp cayenne pepper

2 egg whites

1 ½ lb red snapper fillets

2 cups olive oil

4 kaiser rolls

4 large leaves fresh lettuce

4 slices tomato

Serves 4

Prepare the red pepper aioli.

Preheat the oven to 300°F.

In a shallow stainless steel bowl or pie plate, mix together the flours, salt and cayenne. In a separate small bowl, beat the egg whites thoroughly until frothy, about 2 minutes.

Dredge the snapper fillets in the flour, followed by the egg whites, then back to the flour again to ensure the fish is completely coated in flour.

Heat the oil in a large frying pan over medium heat. Once the oil is hot but not smoking, carefully add one fish fillet at a time and shallow fry for 2 to 3 minutes on the first side, or until golden brown and lightly crisp. Carefully flip the fillet and shallow fry for 2 minutes on the second side. You will likely have to cook the fish in batches to avoid overcrowding the pan. Drain the first batch of excess oil on paper towel and keep the fish warm in the oven while you cook the remainder. A heavy pan is a must for pan-frying fish fillets, so is only turning your fish once, as this helps prevent the fish from becoming soggy or oversaturated in oil. Always use fresh oil, and do not skimp on it.

Slice the rolls in half and toast in the oven for 3 to 4 minutes.

Spread a generous tablespoonful of red pepper aioli on the bottom half of each roll. Add the lettuce and tomato, and then the snapper fillets (1–2 fillets on each, depending on the size). Top with more aioli and then the top half of each roll.

· ·

COOK'S NOTE: *Perfectly good kaiser rolls can be found in the bakery of most supermarkets these days. It's a bit challenging to make them at home because malt powder (one of the key ingredients) is hard to find. If you want to use homemade rolls for the sandwiches, use my recipe for Honey Whole Wheat Buns (page 222).*

Seafood Salad Pita Pockets

This dish makes for a great beach picnic or light supper in the summer when you don't want to heat up the kitchen. Warm pita bread makes it extra special.

¼ cup mayonnaise

3 Tbsp creole mustard (grainy or stoneground are good alternatives)

1 tsp Tabasco sauce

¼ tsp paprika or smoked paprika

¼ tsp ground celery seed

3 Tbsp olive oil

½ lb shrimp (15–20 shrimp), peeled and deveined

½ lb albacore tuna, cut into ½-inch chunks

2 green onions, thinly sliced

1 stalk celery, thinly sliced

¼ apple, julienned (preferably Fuji, Gala or Granny Smith; avoid baking apples, such as Rome, as they are dry)

Salt and pepper

4 pita pocket breads

Serves 4

Make a dressing for the seafood by combining the mayo, mustard, Tabasco, paprika and celery seed in a large bowl. Mix with a fork until incorporated, then set aside.

Heat the oil in a large, heavy-bottomed frying pan over medium-high heat and sear the shrimp for 30 to 45 seconds per side, or until they turn pink. Remove from the pan and set aside. In the same pan, quickly sauté the tuna for about 3 minutes, turning the pieces frequently. You want the fish to be a little crispy on the outside and light red-pink in the inside; if you overcook the tuna it will become dry.

Combine the seafood and spoon it into the dressing. Fold in the green onions, celery and apple. Season to taste with salt and pepper. Cut the pita pockets in half and fill with the seafood salad.

. . . .

COOK'S NOTE: *The key to maximum flavor is spooning the freshly sautéed seafood into the dressing when it's still warm—the fish just drinks it up! Chips on the side are always welcome. I have even been known to put some chips inside my sandwiches . . .*

Summer

Tofino is a paradise in summer, a Goldilocks town—not too cold and not too hot. It's just right. It also feels as if the entire world has moved in, with the town's population swelling from 1,700 to 25,000, and of course, all of them are hungry. Fishermen have a summer saying: "The bite is on!" And is it ever! They're fishing from 5 a.m. until dark every day and night. Fresh salmon, halibut and ling cod surrender to their lines; the farmers' market returns to downtown; the bears compete with berry pickers for the best roadside blackberries; jamming parties overlap with pickling nights; and the little red truck from the Tofino-Ucluelet Culinary Guild tears around from restaurant to restaurant, delivering fresh, organic produce gathered from BC's best farms. It feels like an international village, laid-back, overabundant and uniquely delicious.

BBQ Brisket Sandwich

I was born in Kansas City, but lived in South Florida and Texas for many years. You'll see that my sauce and methods for this recipe are a tasty combination of all three regions' cooking traditions. They're also so versatile that they can be used on brisket, pulled pork, salmon, shrimp and grits. This recipe takes time, as the brisket has to marinate for 2 to 3 days in the refrigerator, but it's well worth the wait! My West Texas Onion Rings (page 212) are a must-have to be served on the side of this brisket, and SoBo Slaw (page 214) makes a really nice addition to the sandwiches. If you can't use the brisket all at once, it can be frozen in its sauce for up to 3 months.

Dry Rub

1 cup packed brown sugar

1 cup salt

1 cup ancho chili powder

½ cup paprika

2 Tbsp cayenne pepper

Brisket

2 cups beef stock

Habanero Whisky BBQ
Sauce (page 118)

1 brisket, 3–5 lb (average size)

10 Honey Whole Wheat Buns
(page 222, or use store-bought
buns of your choice)

Serves up to 10

Combine the sugar, salt, chili powder, paprika and cayenne to create a dry rub. Liberally rub this onto the brisket with your hands. Cover in plastic wrap and marinate the brisket for 2 to 3 days in the fridge.

Before cooking, remove the brisket from the fridge and allow to it come to almost room temperature. Preheat the oven to 275°F.

Place the beef stock with the brisket and 2 cups of the BBQ sauce in a roasting pan, and bring to a boil on the stovetop. Turn off the heat, cover tightly with aluminum foil and place in the oven for 3 ½ to 4 hours. When the brisket is done, the meat should fall apart easily.

Remove the brisket from the oven and then from the roasting pan, and skim off any excess fat from the liquid in the roasting pan. Allow the brisket to cool in its juices until it is easy to handle, 20 to 30 minutes.

Turn the oven up to 350°F.

Trim the brisket of excess fat and then either shred the meat by hand or slice it across the grain (depending on your preference). Just before you are ready to serve it, move the shreds or slices back to the roasting pan with the remaining liquid, and cover the meat with 2 more cups of BBQ sauce. Cover the roasting pan with aluminum foil and reheat in the oven for 10 minutes.

To construct each sandwich, slice open the buns, add a tower of brisket meat and top with BBQ sauce. If you have extra BBQ sauce to spare, it is excellent for dipping our West Texas Onion Rings into.

continued on next page

Habanero Whisky BBQ Sauce

½ cup canola oil

1 medium yellow onion, diced small

1 jalapeño pepper, seeded, diced small

1 red bell pepper, diced small

1 green bell pepper, diced small

4 cloves garlic, minced

2 Tbsp dry mustard

1 ½ Tbsp salt (or to taste)

1 Tbsp ground cumin

¼ cup whisky or bourbon (Jack Daniel's, Maker's Mark, or your choice)

4 cups ketchup

1 cup apple cider vinegar

¾ cup Dijon mustard

¼ cup packed brown sugar

¼ cup molasses

1 tsp ground dried habanero chili powder

Makes 8 cups

Heat the oil in a medium-sized, heavy-bottomed pot over medium heat. Sauté the onion, jalapeño and bell peppers for 20 minutes or until tender, gently stirring with a wooden spoon to prevent burning. Add the garlic, dry mustard, salt and cumin and cook for an additional 2 minutes.

Add the whisky and let it evaporate for 1 minute. Add the ketchup, cider vinegar, Dijon, brown sugar, molasses and chili powder and simmer on low heat for 1 hour, stirring frequently to avoid burning.

Remove from the heat and allow to cool to room temperature.

. . . .

COOK'S NOTE: *This sauce is rooted in the Kansas City–style of sweet ketchup-based sauces, but blended with East Coast vinegar and given a little Texan spice to round it all out. It works beautifully with brisket, onion rings, burgers, chicken, shrimp or grits. It can be stored in a tightly sealed nonreactive glass or plastic container in the fridge for up to 30 days.*

Grilled Veggie Sandwich

Your vegetarian friends will thank you for this at your next BBQ. I've been a big fan of vegetables all my life so this is a well-used recipe around my house. The Portobello mushroom is the meaty part, with the squash adding a sweet dimension, and the onions and peppers a smoky depth that pairs well with the garlicky romesco. It's a very hearty sandwich and doesn't really need chips or sides, maybe just a few broiled olives. If you're in the mood for it, add a slice of provolone cheese.

1 cup Romesco Sauce (page 171)

2 Portobello mushrooms, de-stemmed and left whole

1 small zucchini, sliced lengthwise into 4

1 small yellow squash (I use crookneck), sliced lengthwise into 4

1 red onion, sliced into 4 intact disks

1 red bell pepper, seeded and quartered

4 Tbsp olive oil

2 tsp salt

4 ciabatta buns

Serves 4

Prepare the romesco sauce.

Preheat the BBQ to high.

In a large bowl, mix all the vegetables with 3 Tbsp of the olive oil to coat them evenly, then season with salt. Lay the vegetables on the grill and cook until the grill marks are dark brown but the veggies are still firm. You want to grill them for 2 to 3 minutes on each side.

When the mushroom caps come off the grill, slice them lengthwise. Cut the zucchini and yellow squash slices in three to four pieces per strip (this makes them easier to distribute among the sandwiches).

Cut the ciabatta buns in half, lightly brush them with the remaining 1 Tbsp oil and grill for 2 to 3 minutes on each side, taking care not to burn them.

Spread about 2 Tbsp of the romesco sauce on the bottom half of each bun, layer the veggies on top then spread the remaining romesco sauce on the top half of the bun.

The Great Big Vegan Burger

I'd always wanted to have a good vegan burger on the menu. My cooks and I didn't like the idea of pre-made, frozen patties so we decided to make our own. It only took a couple of days of experimentation before we nailed it. I really like the cumin and coriander in the spice mix, but if you're worried that it might be too strong, leave it out.

Burgers

1 cup dried black beans, rinsed

2 tsp salt

½ cup quinoa

1 large Portobello mushroom cap, diced small

¼ large red onion, diced

1 Tbsp minced garlic (3–4 cloves)

¼ cup plus 2 Tbsp olive oil

1 Tbsp balsamic vinegar

½ cup pumpkin seeds

2 Tbsp whole flaxseeds, ground

½ medium carrot, grated

¼ cup fresh flat-leaf parsley

2 Tbsp lemon juice (1 medium lemon)

1 tsp ground cumin

1 tsp ground coriander

1 tsp chili powder

8 burger buns

Garnish

20–30 leaves fresh spinach (roughly 1 cup)

4 Dill Pickles, sliced lengthwise (page 254)

¾ cup ketchup

2 avocados, sliced

2 large beefsteak or heirloom tomatoes, sliced ½-inch thick

Serves 8

For the burgers, add the beans and 4 cups of cold water to a medium-sized pot over high heat, and bring to a boil. Turn the heat to low, cover and simmer for 2 ½ to 3 hours or until tender. You may need to add more water as they simmer, as you do not want the pot to run dry. When the beans are tender, add 1 tsp of the salt, then drain and allow to cool.

Preheat the oven to 400°F.

Toast the quinoa on a baking sheet in the oven for 5 minutes. Remove from the oven and transfer to a medium-sized saucepan. Add 1 cup of water and bring to a boil. Turn the heat to low, cover and simmer for about 11 minutes, or until the quinoa is light and fluffy. Drain the quinoa of any excess water and let it cool on a baking sheet.

Place the mushroom, onion and garlic on a baking sheet and pour the ¼ cup oil and the vinegar overtop. Roast for 15 minutes. Remove from the oven and set aside to cool.

Toast the pumpkin seeds on a baking sheet in the oven for 5 minutes. Remove from the oven and allow to cool.

Meanwhile, plump the flaxseeds up by soaking them for 10 minutes in a small bowl filled with 6 Tbsp of water. The flaxseeds are the burger's binding agent.

Transfer the beans, quinoa, mushroom mixture, pumpkin seeds, flaxseeds, carrot, parsley, lemon juice and spices, including the remaining 1 tsp of salt, to a large bowl and mix thoroughly. Add half of this mixture to a food processor and pulse for a few seconds until the beans start to break down. You are not looking for a paste, you just want the mixture to bind together so it can be shaped into burgers. Remove and repeat the process with the remaining half of the mixture.

Shape the mixture by hand into eight burger patties. Heat the remaining 2 Tbsp oil in a frying pan over medium-high heat and pan-sear the burgers for 3 minutes on one side. Turn the heat down to medium and sear for another 3 to 4 minutes on the other side. Everything is cooked so you are just heating the burger and adding texture to the outside.

Construct the burgers, adding the garnishes. I like them in the order of bottom bun, spinach, dill pickles, patty, ketchup, avocado, tomato, top bun.

. . . .

COOK'S NOTE: *The biggest challenge with vegan burgers is that they tend to crumble due to the low level of fat in the recipe. If you're not a vegan, feel free to crack an egg in the mixture before pulsing in the food processor. These burgers are a bit time-consuming so I usually feed my family four, and freeze four in a large sealable freezer bag, keeping them flat in the freezer. If you want to do that too, just half the quantities of the garnishes called for in the recipe.*

Appetizers & Snacks
(and one very special drink)

Fresh Oysters with Champagne Mignonette 124

Miso Oysters with Smoked Salmon Bacon 126

Smoked Oyster Spudwich 128

SoBo Ceviche 131

Crab and Goat Cheese Wontons 132

Crab and Corn Fritters 134

Crispy Shrimp Cakes with 900 Island Sauce 135

Vera Cruz Shrimp Cocktail 137

Spicy Cibolo Shrimp with Blue Cheese Dressing 138

Shrimp Cakes with Dungeness Crab, Avocado and Salsa Verde 141

Hippy Chicken 142

Thai Chicken on Roti 145

Risotto Bullets 148

Braeden's Salmon Tofu Pockets 150

Polenta Fries with Caesar Dipping Sauce 152

Sunchoke Hummus 155

Guacamole 156

Cajun Spiced Pecans 157

Broiled Olives 158

SoBo Margarita 161

Fresh Oysters
with Champagne Mignonette

Oysters on the half-shell are a very special treat. My favorite types for eating raw are the small Marina's Top Drawer, Gem, Kushi, Kumamoto and Malpeque. Because they are a personal favorite of mine, I can eat four or five of these (and many of my friends eat six or eight) but most people will eat two or three at a cocktail party. They're not filling, just a wonderful West Coast treat.

Champagne Mignonette (see below)

12 live small oysters (see sidebar page 127)

½ tsp freshly grated horseradish

Makes 12 small oysters on the half-shell (3–4 per person)

Prepare the champagne mignonette. Set aside. (Ideally you should prepare this about 20 minutes before serving to let the onions marinate in the vinegar.)

Scrub all the oysters under cold water with a brush to remove barnacles and excess sand. Shuck the oysters right before serving them (see sidebar). Garnish with horseradish and mignonette.

Champagne Mignonette

⅓ cup champagne vinegar

1 medium shallot, minced

¼ tsp lemon zest

Pepper

Makes ¼ cup

Combine the champagne vinegar, shallots, lemon zest and pepper in a bowl and mix well. This can be stored in an airtight container in the fridge for up to 1 week.

How to Shuck an Oyster

You will need an oyster shucker, two heavy-duty, clean cloths or a glove (to protect your hand) and some patience if you have never shucked before. Place the oyster with the deeper shell facing down in the middle of a folded cloth to hold it steady, or hold it in a gloved hand. At the back of the oyster you'll find a hinge. Slide the oyster knife into that back area next to the hinge and move the shucker back and forth until you feel the natural opening. Twist your wrist a bit in an upward motion until you hear the shell click open. This will take a wee bit of force, so be careful. Slide the shucker very carefully up around the top part and along the side of the shell to loosen it. When you have the top shell off, place it to the side and run your shucker underneath the meaty part of the oyster to loosen it. Keep as much oyster liquid (it's called "liquor") as possible in the shell. Check for shell fragments in the meat. I like to take the top of the shell and use it to steady the bottom shell, thus holding the liquor in. The more shucking you do, the better and more confident you will become. It's a little scary at first. If you have Internet access, check YouTube for some great videos on shucking. Alternatively, visit your local raw oyster bar and observe the pros at work while you enjoy a glass of champagne.

The Out Landish Shellfish Guild
DISCOVERY ISLANDS, BC

My introduction to the Out Landish Shellfish Guild came out of the blue when Kathy McLaggan showed up at SoBo one day with a bag of oysters in her hand for me to try. She was soaked to the bone by a Tofino storm, so I invited her in. Before long I knew she was exactly the sort of person I wanted to source my food from. Since that day, almost all the shellfish we use in the restaurant has come from the fine farmers of Out Landish.

Out Landish's story is a good one. Before the Guild formed, most of its farmer-members were working independently, selling to major buyers. Then prices dropped so low that they were being forced to sell oysters at a loss. They realized they needed to either band together or give up their operations entirely. Thankfully they chose the first option.

Today, Out Landish includes Kathy and Victor McLaggan, Jules Frank and Ian Mowat, Troy Bouchard, Mike Gibbons, Clarke Leggett and Michael McLean. They work farms and beaches in the Discovery Islands area, which has some of the West Coast's cleanest and richest waters. Nestled between the mainland and Vancouver Island, they have a truly special way of life. "The best kind of day is when you show up at the beach in the spring, on an outgoing tide," Victor McLaggan told me. "The sun is shining, the sea is calm and you can smell the seaweed. The clams are spitting and the oysters have a fresh new translucent frill. There's not much that's better than that."

Miso Oysters
with Smoked Salmon Bacon

Rich, salty and spicy—these babies hit all the right notes! They're a staple on the SoBo menu. Due to the rich nature of this dish, two to three oysters are about all anyone can eat. I use medium-sized Beach oysters for broiling as their shells are harder than those of the small, delicate Tray oysters, so they don't crack on the grill like the small varieties do.

Miso Sauce (page 127)

8 slices cold-smoked salmon

8 medium oysters

Serves 4

Prepare the miso sauce.

Preheat the oven to 300°F. Place a wire rack on top of a baking sheet and spray it with cooking spray.

Lay the salmon in a row across the prepared wire rack. Bake until dried out but not burned, around 8 minutes (it will start to smell like bacon). Take the salmon off the rack and let cool for 2 to 3 minutes.

Turn the oven up to 400°F.

Place the oysters on a baking sheet and bake for 3 minutes. This will make the oysters easier to pop open. Shuck the oysters (see page 124). The oysters will be hot and full of liquor so take extra care shucking. You can certainly shuck them before roasting, but oysters exposed to heat will start to loosen on their own, making them easier to open. Place the shucked oysters back on the baking sheet. Set aside the top shells.

Place one slice of salmon bacon and 2 Tbsp miso sauce on top of each oyster. Return to the oven and bake until very bubbly and golden brown. The broiler setting is a great way to achieve a brûlée top, but watch over the oysters carefully as they can burn quickly.

If you prefer to use a BBQ, lay the oysters directly on the rack over high heat and try to space them out a bit so shards of cracked shell don't end up all over the oysters. You will know it's done when the miso gets bubbly and starts to turn dark brown, about 5 minutes.

To serve, turn the empty top shells upside down, and use them to balance the broiled oyster on top—they act as a good leveling device to rest the broiled oyster on so the filling doesn't run out of the shell. Serve two oysters per person.

Miso Sauce

1 egg yolk

1 Tbsp white miso paste

1 Tbsp rice vinegar

½ Tbsp sambal oelek (or chili garlic sauce)

¾ cup canola oil

Makes 1 cup

Combine all the ingredients, except the oil, in a medium-sized bowl and whisk gently to combine. Add the oil slowly, whisking until the dressing has emulsified. Refrigerate for up to 2 days.

Live Oysters

It's key to keep oysters alive until you're ready to serve them. I put my oysters with the deeper shell facing down, as flat as possible, covered with a damp towel in the fridge for 3 to 4 days. Keeping them very cold is best. If an oyster is open, it is already dead and you need to discard it. Oysters should smell like the sea. The smell of a bad oyster is hard to mistake.

Smoked Oyster Spudwich

To say that Artie and I love oysters is an understatement—we just can't get enough of them. We entered this recipe in the 2004 Clayoquot Oyster Festival and won the People's Choice Award. It's super-easy if you can find a great-quality smoked oyster.

20 gourmet-quality (hard and thick) potato chips

1 avocado, mashed

Two 6 oz cans smoked oysters (I recommend the Oyster Man brand)

1 cup SoBo Slaw (page 214)

Makes 10 canapés (most people will enjoy 1 or 2 each)

Build a sandwich starting with one chip. Slather it with avocado, add a smoked oyster and some slaw and top with another chip. This appetizer is intended to be eaten in one or two bites.

SoBo Ceviche

The last thing you want to do on a summer day is spend a lot of time in a hot kitchen. This dish requires no heat and is so quick and easy (although it needs to be prepped a couple of hours in advance) that you can get right back outside to enjoy the sunshine. This recipe is a lazy Sunday favorite in my household. Ceviche is best eaten within 12 hours of preparation, so keep your batches small. Using only the freshest seafood available is key.

½ lb halibut, diced small

¼ lb spot prawns or large shrimp, peeled and deveined, diced small

¼ lb scallops, diced small

1 ½ cups lime juice (preferably key lime) (about 40 key limes or 16 limes)

2 serrano chilies, seeded, diced small

½ avocado, diced small

½ Roma tomato, seeded, diced small

¼ medium red bell pepper, diced small

1 green onion, thinly sliced

¼ cup chopped fresh cilantro

1 ½ tsp salt

1 Tbsp extra virgin olive oil

1 head gem lettuce (or you can use baby romaine or baby Bibb leaves) or 4 cups tortilla chips

Serves 6–8

Combine the halibut, prawns, scallops and lime juice in a medium-sized bowl and marinate for 2 to 3 hours in the refrigerator. The marinating is the cooking—the citric acid in the lime juice changes the texture of the fish to that of cooked while retaining the "raw" taste—no heat is used.

Drain off the lime juice and discard. Carefully fold in the chilies, avocado, tomato, peppers, green onions, cilantro and salt. Keep the ceviche well chilled until you are ready to serve.

To serve, drizzle the extra virgin olive oil over the ceviche and use the gem lettuce leaves or tortilla chips to scoop it up and enjoy.

· ·

COOK'S NOTE: *Dicing all the seafood into a uniform size will ensure it marinates evenly. Dice the vegetables a little smaller than the seafood.*

Crab and Goat Cheese Wontons

These are pillows of salty goodness. I don't usually pair seafood with cheese, but crab is an exception. Artie and I used to go to a restaurant in Rhinecliff, New York, called China Rose and there we fell in love with a dish that inspired this recipe. The Cilantro Jalapeño Dipping Sauce really sets it off.

Cilantro Jalapeño Dipping
Sauce (see below)

1 cup cooked crabmeat (see page 194, or use store-bought fresh crab, not canned, Dungeness if available)

½ cup fresh goat cheese

2 green onions, thinly sliced

16 wonton wrappers

1 egg, well beaten

2 large cabbage leaves (any type)

Makes 16 wontons (serves 4)

Prepare the cilantro jalapeño dipping sauce and set aside.

In a large bowl, fold the crab, cheese and green onions together. Place 2 tsp of the mixture in the center of each wonton wrapper. Dip your fingers in the beaten egg and run them around the wonton corners before twisting them closed around the mixture. The egg wash acts as a glue.

Place a bamboo steamer with two cabbage leaves in it over a pot of boiling water. In two equal batches, arrange the wontons on top of the cabbage. Cover and steam the wontons for 2 to 3 minutes. Remove the wontons and serve hot with the cilantro jalapeño dipping sauce.

Cilantro Jalapeño Dipping Sauce

1 ½ cups plain yogurt

1 jalapeño pepper, seeded and diced

½ cup chopped fresh cilantro

¼ cup lime juice (2 medium limes)

1 tsp salt

Makes 2 cups

Whisk all the ingredients together in a bowl. The sauce will keep in an airtight container in the fridge for 48 hours.

Crab and Corn Fritters

Fritters are basically just batter with a little filling inside. They're crispy, light and fun

1 ½ cups flour

½ Tbsp baking powder

½ Tbsp salt

2 Tbsp olive oil

1 egg, separated

Remoulade Sauce (see below)

½ cup cooked crabmeat (see page 194, or use store-bought)

¾ cup corn kernels (frozen and thawed is fine)

1 green onion, sliced

½ jalapeño pepper, diced

3 cups canola oil

Serves 4–6

Stir together the flour, baking powder and salt. Add the olive oil and ¾ cup water, a little at a time. Add the egg yolk and stir until the batter achieves a smooth consistency.

In a medium-sized bowl, beat the egg white until just stiff, 3 to 4 minutes. Fold the egg whites together gently with the batter and refrigerate for 1 hour.

While the batter is in the fridge, prepare the remoulade sauce. Once the batter is cool, fold in the crabmeat with the corn, green onions and jalapeño.

Heat the canola oil in a deep saucepan over medium-high heat. Very carefully drop about 2 Tbsp of batter into the oil. Fry the fritters for 3 to 4 minutes in total, turning them as they fry, until golden brown. Serve right away with remoulade sauce on the side for dipping.

Remoulade Sauce

1 egg, hard-boiled and peeled

1 clove garlic, minced

1 Tbsp white wine vinegar

2 tsp Dijon mustard

2 tsp mayonnaise

1 tsp Worcestershire sauce

1 drop Tabasco sauce

1 tsp minced capers

1 tsp minced flat-leaf parsley

1 tsp minced tarragon

1 tsp minced chervil

1 tsp minced gherkins

Makes ½ cup

Combine the egg with the garlic, vinegar, mustard, mayonnaise, Worcestershire sauce and Tabasco sauce, mixing well. Fold in the capers, parsley, tarragon, chervil and gherkins and mix well. Refrigerate for up to 4 days.

Crispy Shrimp Cakes with 900 Island Sauce

This recipe is an adaptation of the one my mentor, Melissa Kelly, made at the Old Chatham Sheepherding Company Inn in upstate New York back in the 1990s. It's always a crowd-pleaser, especially with the 900 Island Sauce (like the ubiquitous Thousand Island dressing but without the sweet relish). The shrimp cakes can be served with a side salad for an elegant lunch, or as appetizers at a cocktail party. You can easily substitute crab for the shrimp or blend the two together.

900 Island Sauce (see below)

¼ cup butter

1 large yellow onion, diced small

¼ medium red bell pepper, diced small

¼ medium green bell pepper, diced small

1 jalapeño pepper, seeded, diced small

1 Tbsp salt

2 tsp dry mustard

1 tsp dried oregano

1 tsp dried basil

1 tsp dried thyme

¼ cup flour

½ cup whipping cream

4 egg yolks

1 lb baby shrimp

2 cups Panko breadcrumbs

4 egg whites, lightly beaten

1 cup peanut oil

Serves 8

Make the 900 Island sauce.

Heat the butter in a medium-sized, heavy-bottomed saucepan over medium heat and add the onion, peppers, jalapeños, salt, dry mustard and dried herbs. Sauté for 15 minutes, stirring frequently with a wooden spoon. Add the flour, turn the heat to low and cook for an additional 4 minutes, stirring constantly (this is important as the mixture will start to burn otherwise)—you are creating a roux, or thicker. Slowly add the cream while continuing to stir. When the mixture begins to pull away from the sides of the pan, take the pan off the heat and stir in the egg yolks one at a time.

Allow the mixture to cool for 15 minutes. When it has cooled, add the shrimp and half the breadcrumbs. Use your hands (or a small ice cream scoop) to divide the mixture into 16 golf-ball sized balls. Form them into thick cakes.

Add the egg whites to a small bowl, and the remainder of the breadcrumbs to another bowl. This is your breading station: dip each cake into the egg whites and then dredge it in the breadcrumbs.

Heat the oil in a medium-sized, heavy-bottomed saucepan over medium-high heat and fry the cakes in batches for about 1 ½ minutes per side or until golden brown. Place the cakes on paper towel to soak up excess oil. Serve drizzled with 900 Island sauce.

....

COOK'S NOTE: *If you are making the cakes in advance, they can be refrigerated and then reheated on a baking sheet at 350°F for 4 to 5 minutes.*

900 Island Sauce

¼ cup Dijon mustard

¼ cup mayonnaise

¼ cup sour cream

2 Tbsp grainy mustard

2 Tbsp ketchup

In a medium-sized bowl, combine all the ingredients and whisk well. This sauce will keep in the fridge for 1 week. It is also great on ham and cheese sandwiches, fried oysters or even french fries.

Makes 1 cup

Veracruz Shrimp Cocktail

This is my take on what would happen if the classic 1960s Vegas shrimp cocktail met the more authentic Mexican type and they moved into a bowl together. The sauce is a little like a thick Bloody Mary, only we use shrimp instead of vodka (I've actually tried it with vodka, though, and it's pretty darn good!). Like the ceviche on page 131, this recipe needs to be prepped a couple of hours before you plan to serve it.

Seafood Cocktail Sauce (see below)

1 lb baby shrimp (precooked)

½ cucumber, diced

½ cup chopped fresh cilantro

½ avocado, diced

1 green onion, chopped

Serves 4

Prepare the seafood cocktail sauce.

In a medium-sized bowl, gently combine the baby shrimp, cucumber, cilantro, avocado and green onions. Divide the shrimp mixture between four bowls, and pour the cocktail sauce overtop before serving.

....

COOK'S NOTE: *If you tire of shrimp, fresh crabmeat makes for a wonderful substitution or addition, if you would like to combine the two. Just keep the overall amount of seafood in the recipe to about 1 lb. Clamato juice is a tomato juice with the addition of a little clam juice. You can use V-8 if Clamato juice is not available where you are.*

Seafood Cocktail Sauce

3 cups Clamato juice (see Cook's Note)

2 cups small-diced tomatoes
(2–3 medium tomatoes)

2 cups puréed roasted red
bell peppers (page 252)

½ cup ketchup

2 Tbsp freshly grated horseradish

½ jalapeño pepper, finely diced

2 Tbsp lemon juice (1 medium lemon)

2 tsp Worcestershire sauce

2 tsp salt

1 tsp pepper

1 tsp Tabasco sauce

Makes 8 cups

Place all the ingredients in a pitcher. Stir everything together gently using a wooden spoon. Chill in the fridge for at least 2 hours before using. Refrigerate for up to 4 days.

Spicy Cibolo Shrimp
with Blue Cheese Dressing

This dish was inspired by the hot Louisiana-style "buffalo" chicken wing craze of the 1980s. I came up with it while cooking at Cibolo Creek Ranch in Texas (*cibolo* means "buffalo" in Spanish) and I'm still cooking it every day. This pairs very well with a freshly squeezed lime margarita (page 161) or an icy cold lager beer.

Tequila Cayenne Sauce (see below)

1 cup Blue Cheese Dressing (page 139)

1 cup corn flour

1 cup flour

1 Tbsp salt

2 tsp cayenne pepper

20 shrimp or large prawns, peeled and deveined

1 cup buttermilk

6 cups canola oil

20 leaves Bibb lettuce

2 tsp crumbled blue cheese

6 sprigs fresh dill

3 limes, quartered

Serves 4

Prepare the tequila cayenne sauce and blue cheese dressing.

Mix together the flours, salt and cayenne in a medium-sized bowl, and set aside. In a separate medium-sized bowl, soak the shrimp in the buttermilk for 5 minutes.

In a heavy-bottomed deep pot (or deep-fryer), add the canola oil and heat to 325°F. Test that the oil is hot by adding a cube of bread to the pan. It should instantly start to sizzle and should turn golden brown within 1 to 1 ½ minutes. It's important to have the correct temperature for frying or you could ruin a lot of costly shrimp.

Remove the shrimp from the buttermilk and toss each one in the flour mixture, coating liberally.

Working in batches, add the coated shrimp to the hot oil for about 1 minute or until golden brown. Be careful not to overcrowd the pan. Scoop out the shrimp and place them on paper towel to soak up any excess oil.

In a small bowl, place the tequila cayenne sauce and coat each fried shrimp liberally. Divide the lettuce leaves between four plates and serve the shrimp on a bed of lettuce leaves. Top each one with ½ tsp crumbled blue cheese. Garnish with fresh dill and a squeeze of lime. Serve with blue cheese dressing for dipping.

Tequila Cayenne Sauce

¼ cup salted butter

½ cup minced garlic (2–2 ½ heads)

½ cup Louisiana-style hot sauce (I like Frank's RedHot)

1 Tbsp tequila

1 Tbsp lime juice (1 medium lime)

Melt the butter in a deep pot over low heat and sweat the garlic for 10 minutes. Whisk in the hot sauce, then add the tequila (be very careful at this point as it could ignite). Gently cook off the alcohol for 3 to 4 minutes, and finish by mixing in the lime juice. Remove from the heat and set aside. Refrigerate for up to 1 week.

Makes ¾ cup

Blue Cheese Dressing

¼ cup crumbled blue cheese

¼ cup mayonnaise

¼ cup sour cream

1 tsp lemon juice

1 tsp Worcestershire sauce

¼ tsp Tabasco sauce

⅛ tsp salt

⅛ tsp pepper

2 tsp milk (optional)

Makes 1 cup

Combine all the ingredients, except the milk, in a food processor and blend for 1 minute. If you like your dressing a little thinner, add the milk. Refrigerate for up to 5 days.

. . . .

COOK'S NOTE: *As Artie explains to SoBo diners, there are specific rules for enjoying this dish: pick up the lettuce leaf and shrimp* together, *top with the desired amount of dressing and then pop in your mouth. The lettuce is essential to cool down the spicy nature of the shrimp.*

Shrimp Cakes
with Dungeness Crab, Avocado and Salsa Verde

This is an upscale version of the shrimp cake. The addition of crabmeat, avocado and Salsa Verde makes for a solid lunch or an impressive starter for a dinner party. The cakes, crab and salsa can be made in advance so if you're having guests it's a snap at serving time.

Crispy Shrimp Cakes (page135)

1 cup cooked crabmeat (see page 194, or use store-bought fresh crab, not canned, Dungeness if available)

1 avocado, cut into 12 slices

Salsa Verde (see below)

Serves 4

Prepare the crispy shrimp cakes, but divide the mixture into 4 baseball-sized balls (instead of 16 "golf balls") and shape them into hockey-puck–sized cakes. If necessary, you can prepare and fry them an hour or so in advance, then reheat them in the oven before serving (10 minutes at 350°F).

Split each shrimp cake in half through the middle like a burger bun. Layer the bottom with ¼ cup crabmeat and 3 slices of avocado and place the top of the shrimp cake back on top to create a small sandwich.

Spoon ¼ cup salsa onto each plate and place the crabmeat and shrimp cake in the middle.

Salsa Verde

10 fresh tomatillos, cleaned and core removed (see Cook's Note)

2 jalapeño peppers, stemmed

1 tsp minced garlic (1–2 cloves)

¼ cup fresh cilantro leaves

¼ cup lime juice (2 medium limes)

2 Tbsp sugar

1 Tbsp salt

Makes 1 cup

Preheat the oven to 450°F. Line a baking sheet with parchment paper or aluminum foil.

Place the tomatillos and jalapeños on the prepared baking sheet. Roast for 10 minutes on one side then turn and roast for an additional 5 to 10 minutes on the other, or until the tomatillos blacken and cook down a bit. They will start to deflate and the juices will run onto the pan, which is why I suggest using parchment or foil. It makes cleaning easier and reserves the juices.

In a food processor, blend the tomatillos and their juices with the jalapeños, garlic, cilantro, lime juice, sugar and salt until smooth.

....

COOK'S NOTE: *The tomatillos in this salsa will have a papery husk on the exterior and can be very sticky on the outside, so remove the husks and wash the tomatillos well to get all the sticky residue off. This salsa is lovely when warm but room temperature is also just fine. I try not to serve it cold just out of the fridge as it is more gelatinous and just doesn't taste as good!*

Hippy Chicken

This recipe—one of my favorites—was featured in *The Gourmet Cookbook*, edited by Ruth Reichl. Word is the magazine's test kitchen had to make a second batch on the fly because the testers gobbled down the first batch so quickly. Once you try it, you'll understand why! It's such a versatile recipe: I love it hot from the frying pan, and it's also excellent to make in advance and refrigerate overnight. It's a casual dish that's great to share with family and friends, and is guaranteed to shine at an outdoor picnic—I usually serve it in one big bowl and let everyone fight over it! The chicken needs to marinate for at least 8 hours in the fridge (24 hours is even better) so plan ahead when making it.

½ cup packed light brown sugar

½ cup apple cider vinegar

½ cup lemon juice (2 large lemons)

½ cup soy sauce

¼ cup puréed canned chipotle chilies in adobo sauce

1 tsp dry mustard

4 cloves garlic, minced

1 ½ lb boneless chicken (thigh, breasts or both), cut into strips, 1 ½ inches thick

¼ cup almonds

¼ cup pumpkin seeds

¼ cup sunflower seeds

¼ cup hemp seeds

2 Tbsp sesame seeds

Pinch cayenne pepper

¼ cup unbleached organic flour

4 eggs

¼ cup butter

1 cup vegetable oil

2 Tbsp salt (optional)

Serves 4

In a large bowl mix together the brown sugar, cider vinegar, lemon juice, soy sauce, chipotle chilies, dry mustard and garlic. Place the chicken in a nonreactive baking dish or bowl, or a sealable plastic bag, and pour the mixture overtop. Cover and refrigerate for at least 8 hours, but 24 hours is best.

When you are ready to start cooking, pulse the almonds and seeds in a food processor to chop them until they are the size of breadcrumbs. Transfer them to a large mixing bowl and add the cayenne pepper, mixing by hand to combine, and then the flour, mixing by hand to combine.

In a separate bowl whisk the eggs.

Melt the butter with the oil in a medium-sized frying pan over medium-high heat.

Dip each piece of marinated chicken into the bowl of egg wash then dredge it in the flour mixture. Coat each piece just before you're going to fry it to keep the crust intact. If you coat the chicken and let it sit before frying, the breading will fall off when you try to turn the pieces in the pan.

Using tongs, carefully place the chicken in the hot frying pan. If you don't hear a sizzle the temperature is too low and the chicken will absorb too much oil, so turn up the heat. Fry the pieces for 3 to 4 minutes then turn and fry for another 3 to 4 minutes on the other side, or until golden brown. (If you prefer to deep-fry the chicken, submerge the pieces in hot oil, 325°F, for 3 to 4 minutes and make sure not to overcrowd the fryer.) Move the pieces around a bit to ensure even cooking. If the chicken is browning quickly and the inside remains underdone, you can move it to a baking sheet and finish it in a 400°F degree oven for 4 to 5 minutes.

When the chicken is cooked, remove it from the frying pan and place it on paper towel to soak up any excess oil. If you like it saltier, add the salt now, while the chicken is still hot, so that it sticks.

Thai Chicken on Roti

Thai chicken has been on the SoBo menu for 10 years and we could never take it off without seriously disappointing some regulars. This dish has to be marinated for 24 hours, so plan ahead if you're making it. In the restaurant we serve this with a side of SoBo Slaw (page 214) and let customers decide whether to wrap it up in the roti with the chicken, or have it on the side. We also let them dictate the amount of Peanut Sauce they get! The Thai Chicken also tastes great on its own.

1 cup soy sauce

4-inch piece fresh ginger, minced

¼ cup lime juice (2 medium limes)

2 Tbsp brown sugar

2 Tbsp minced garlic (6–8 cloves)

1 lb bone-in skin-on chicken thighs

Roti (page 146)

Peanut Sauce (page 146)

Serves 8

In a medium-sized bowl, whisk the soy sauce, ginger, lime juice, sugar and garlic together to create a marinade (you'll have about 1 ½ cups). Submerge the chicken in the marinade and marinate for 24 hours in the fridge.

Preheat the oven to 375°F.

In a casserole dish, arrange the chicken thighs and cover them with 1 cup of the marinade. Bake for 25 to 30 minutes, until cooked through. The skin will look burned but this is just the sugar and soy coming out. Remove from the oven and allow to cool.

While the chicken is in the oven, prepare the peanut sauce. Prepare the roti just before serving as it is best served warm. It cools down quickly and doesn't reheat well without getting crispy.

Once the chicken is cool enough to handle, tear it off the bone by hand, and shred the meat, still using your hands. Serve the chicken on the roti, smeared with peanut sauce.

continued on next page

Peanut Sauce

½ cup sweet chili sauce

¼ cup soy sauce

¼ cup lime juice (2 medium limes)

2 medium shallots, minced

1-inch piece fresh ginger, minced

1 Tbsp puréed canned chipotle chilies in adobo sauce

1 Tbsp brown sugar

1 Tbsp molasses

1 Tbsp red wine vinegar

½ cup smooth or chunky peanut butter

½ cup canola oil

2 tsp sesame oil

Makes 2 cups

In a food processor, combine the chili and soy sauces with the lime juice, shallots, ginger, sugar, chipotle chilies, sugar, molasses and vinegar, and pulse until smooth. Add the peanut butter and then, while the machine is running, slowly drizzle in the oils to emulsify the sauce. The sauce can be refrigerated for up to 2 weeks.

Roti

2 cups lukewarm water (warm to the touch but not hot, about 110°F)

3 cups flour, plus extra for kneading

1 ½ tsp salt

Makes 8 roti

Pour the water into a large bowl. Stir in the flour and salt with a wooden spoon. When stirring becomes difficult, turn the dough out onto a lightly floured work surface.

Knead the dough until it feels smooth to the touch. Add a minimal amount of extra flour (if needed) to prevent the dough from sticking to your hands or the countertop. Place the bowl over the dough and let it rest for 10 minutes to relax the gluten.

Divide the dough into eight pieces. On a floured surface, use a rolling pin to roll out each piece of dough as thinly as possible, adding flour as needed to prevent sticking.

Heat a 10-inch or 12-inch cast iron frying pan over high heat. There is no need to oil the pan.

Place the dough pieces one at a time into the hot pan. Cook for 30 to 45 seconds on the first side and then flip to the other side for another 30 seconds or so. The roti will start to fill with air pockets and turn golden brown in spots. Take care not to overcook the roti as it will crack, and you want it to be pliable so you can fold it.

Lyle Young

COWICHAN BAY, BC

When Artie and I moved to Vancouver Island, we knew the coast had some amazing producers, but we didn't know many of them. Sinclair Philip of the Sooke Harbour House and Mara Jernigan of Fairburn Farm were instrumental in connecting us with some of the area's most dedicated farmers. One of the first we met was Lyle Young, of Island Farmhouse Poultry. His family farm in the beautiful Cowichan Valley has been around since the 1900s, making him a fourth-generation chicken farmer. Sourcing meat from animals that have been treated with dignity is very important to me, and I've always been impressed with Lyle's methods.

Lyle works with what's referred to as pasture-raised poultry—meaning his chickens live and feed on real grass in a real pasture. Large moving pens are shifted every few hours to ensure there's always fresh ground beneath the animals. I've often heard them joked about as "Poultry RVs," but it makes such a difference for the life of a meat bird. It's a quality life.

In 2004, a few years after the last poultry processing plant closed on the Island, Lyle opened his own, giving us Island folk another source of good food closer to home—not to mention giving small-scale farmers in the area an opportunity to get their meat to market. I've been a loyal customer for over a decade, and look forward to another decade to come.

Risotto Bullets

These little beauties—one of the most popular items on our menu for years, especially with kids—are a cross between a jalapeño popper and Italian *arancini*.

2 cups Pomodoro Sauce (page 149)

3 cups small-diced assorted mushrooms (preferably Portobello, shiitake or morels)

½ cup olive oil

½ large leek, minced

2 medium shallots, minced

2 Tbsp minced garlic (6–8 cloves)

3 cups uncooked arborio rice

½ cup dry white wine

8 cups hot Vegetable Stock (page 250)

2 tsp salt

1 ½ cups finely grated Asiago cheese

1 lb fontina cheese

6 egg whites, beaten

6 cups dried breadcrumbs

2 cups canola oil

Serves 10

Prepare the pomodoro sauce.

Preheat the oven to 400°F.

Lay the mushrooms on a baking sheet. Drizzle ¼ cup of the olive oil onto the mushrooms and roast in the oven for 20 minutes. Remove from the oven and set aside.

In a medium-sized saucepan over medium-high heat, sauté the leeks, shallots and garlic in the remaining ¼ cup olive oil for 5 minutes until translucent. Add the rice and toast it lightly for 3 to 5 minutes, stirring constantly but slowly with a wooden spoon.

Add the white wine and stir until it is absorbed into the rice. Ladle in 2 cups of stock. Stir the rice gently until it has absorbed most of the liquid. Add another 2 cups of stock, stir until it has been absorbed and repeat, stirring continuously, until most of the stock has been absorbed. Add the salt. This process should take 20 to 25 minutes in total. Remove from the heat when done. The rice should be *al dente* but slightly creamy.

Fold in the mushrooms and Asiago cheese. Allow to cool uncovered in the pot for 1 hour.

While the risotto cools, cut the fontina into strips 1 inch long, ¼ inch wide and ¼ inch thick.

To make a bullet, scoop up enough risotto to cover most of the palm of your hand, lay a piece of cheese in the middle and mold the rice to form a bullet-shaped rice ball around it. The idea is to encase all the fontina so it does not ooze out before the bullet is hot and crispy. Repeat until you have 20 bullets, each about 2 inches long and 1 inch in diameter.

Place the egg whites and breadcrumbs in separate shallow bowls. This is your breading station.

Dip each bullet one at a time into the egg white to coat completely and then lightly dredge in breadcrumbs.

Heat the oil in a medium-sized saucepan over medium heat. Test that the oil is hot enough by adding a cube of bread to the pan. It should instantly start to sizzle and should turn golden brown within 1 to 1 ½ minutes. In batches, being careful not to crowd the pan, fry the bullets for 2 to 3 minutes in total, turning once for even browning. (If you have a deep-fryer, use the 325°F setting and fry until golden brown, around 3 minutes.)

Lay the bullets on paper towel to soak up any excess oil. Lightly salt them and serve with hot pomodoro sauce for dipping.

Pomodoro Sauce

½ cup olive oil

¼ large yellow onion, minced

2 Tbsp minced garlic (6–8 cloves)

One 28 oz can San Marzano or high-quality Italian tomatoes, crushed (I do this with my hands)

1 Tbsp sugar

1 Tbsp salt

1 Tbsp red wine vinegar

¼ cup torn fresh basil leaves

Makes 4 cups

Heat the oil in a heavy-bottomed saucepot over medium-high heat. Sauté the onion and garlic for 3 to 4 minutes to soften without browning.

Add the tomatoes, sugar, salt and vinegar. Cook uncovered on low heat, stirring frequently with a wooden spoon, for about 1 hour. When you are ready to turn off the heat, add the fresh basil.

. . . .

COOK'S NOTE: *This sauce will keep in an airtight container in the fridge for 1 week, and is great to use on pastas and pizzas. It also freezes beautifully for up to 6 months.*

Braeden's Salmon Tofu Pockets

These pockets—named in honor of a special little Tofitian boy—came about one winter evening as we were trying out different styles of tofu for miso soup and came across a pressed tofu that opened up like a pita pocket. It was a bit too sweet for the miso application but we had some sushi rice on hand and decided to play around with these little pouches, stuffing them with salmon. The following recipe clicked like a light switch.

Sushi Rice (page 182)

2 Tbsp sesame oil

2 Tbsp wasabi powder

¼ cup mayonnaise

1 avocado, thinly sliced

1 lb thinly sliced cold-smoked salmon or lox

20 pressed tofu pockets (usually 1 bag, available at Japanese and specialty food stores)

2 Tbsp sesame seeds

2 cups sunflower sprouts

2 Tbsp soy sauce

Serves 8

Prepare the sushi rice.

Add the sesame oil to a small bowl, and oil your hands so that it is easier to work with the rice. Use your hands to shape the rice into 20 disks. Your goal is to make the disks the diameter of a $1 coin (about 1 ¼ inches wide) and about ¾ inch thick. Lay the disks on a clean work surface: this is the start of your assembly line.

In a small bowl, mix the wasabi powder with 1 tsp of water to form a paste. Then combine the wasabi paste with the mayonnaise and spread a small dollop on each rice disk. Add slices of avocado and smoked fish on top (the wasabi mayo acts as a glue to hold the avocado and fish in the pocket).

Gently open the tofu pockets and stuff them with the rice disks. When all the pockets are stuffed, sprinkle them with sesame seeds and top each with a few sprouts. Right before serving, squirt about ¼ tsp soy sauce into each pocket.

A nice wooden sushi rice bowl is lovely to serve these in, but any wide, flat vessel will do.

· ·

COOK'S NOTE: *If the pockets look familiar, it might be because I shared the recipe with the Cactus Club in 2008 and it remains on the menu of some locations to this day.*

Polenta Fries
with Caesar Dipping Sauce

When we opened the SoBo food truck in 2003 I was bound and determined not to cave in to the constant requests for french fries, as most trucks in those days standardly served chips, hot dogs and burgers. We wanted to do something different. We started with salads made from greens from a local farm, fish tacos made with premium halibut and wild salmon, homemade soups, etc. One of our salads was a Caesar salad with polenta croutons—a very popular item in the South. One day as I was explaining to a customer that we did not serve fries, my husband looked at me and asked, "Why don't you make your croutons into fries?" I laughed at him and said it would never work. Boy, was I ever wrong! They are one of the most popular items on the menu, and now a decade later I see them on menus everywhere. Now when people ask if we serve fries, we say, "We sure do."

2 cups milk

1 cup cold water

1 Tbsp salt

1 ½ cups coarse cornmeal

2 Tbsp cold butter, cubed

½ cup grated Parmesan cheese

Caesar Dipping Sauce (page 154)

2 cups canola oil

Serves 10

Preheat the oven to 300°F.

In large, ovenproof saucepan over medium heat, add the milk, water and salt. Cover with an ovenproof lid and cook for 20 to 25 minutes, or until the milk is frothy like a latte. Watch it carefully to avoid scalding the milk. Very slowly add 1 cup of the cornmeal, whisking constantly until smooth. Place the lid back on the saucepan and put it into the oven for 20 minutes, stirring once after 10 minutes.

Remove the polenta from the oven and stir in the butter, then the cheese, using a wooden spoon. Quickly spread the polenta onto a 9- × 13-inch rimmed baking sheet (the rims are important) and refrigerate for 2 hours (when the polenta has completely cooled wrap it in plastic wrap to prevent it from drying out).

Meanwhile, prepare the Caesar dipping sauce.

Cut the cooled polenta into 27 stick-shaped rectangles (1 inch wide by about 4 inches long). I cut them in the baking pan using a paring knife.

Heat the oil in a medium-sized frying pan until it reaches about 300°F. Use a thermometer or test the heat with a bread cube—it should turn golden brown within 1 ½ minutes; if it doesn't, turn up the heat.

continued on next page

Lightly dust the remaining ½ cup cornmeal over all sides of the polenta sticks and fry for 2 to 3 minutes, turning once for even browning. If you have a deep-fryer, use the 325°F setting and fry until the polenta is golden brown, about 3 minutes. Soak the excess oil from the polenta using paper towel, then lightly salt.

You can either serve these in one big bowl, with the Caesar dipping sauce on the side, or (what I like to do) divide the sauce between small bowls and stand the polenta sticks up in the sauce—that way everyone has their own portable dipping station.

. . . .

COOK'S NOTE: *If you do not want to use the whole tray of polenta for fries, you can cut larger squares to create polenta cakes. Brush them lightly with olive oil and grill for 2 minutes on each side for a wonderful cake that can be topped with grilled vegetables and Romesco Sauce (page 171), or served alongside BBQ Brisket Sandwich (page 117).*

Caesar Dipping Sauce

4 anchovies, mashed

2 medium shallots, minced

2 egg yolks

2 Tbsp puréed Roasted Garlic (page 252)

2 Tbsp balsamic vinegar

2 Tbsp Dijon mustard

2 Tbsp lemon juice (1 medium lemon)

2 Tbsp lime juice (1 medium lime)

1 Tbsp puréed canned chipotle chilies in adobo sauce

¼ tsp salt

¼ tsp Worcestershire sauce

3–4 drops Tabasco sauce

Pinch cayenne pepper

2 cups canola oil

1 cup olive oil

Makes 4 cups

In a large, stainless steel bowl, whisk together the anchovies, shallots, egg yolks, garlic, balsamic vinegar, mustard, lemon and lime juices, chipotles, salt, Worcestershire sauce, Tabasco and cayenne pepper. Add the oils slowly, whisking until the dressing has emulsified. This sauce will keep in the fridge for 3 days.

Sunchoke Hummus

We love to add sunchokes to the basic hummus ingredients of chickpeas (aka garbanzo beans), garlic, tahini and lemon. Their sultry, nutty flavor just elevates hummus to a new level and makes it so much more interesting. (Note that the chickpeas need to be soaked overnight.)

1 cup dried chickpeas

½ lb sunchokes (about 1 cup)

¾ cup extra virgin olive oil

¼ cup minced garlic (10–12 cloves)

¼ cup Roasted Garlic (page 252)

¼ cup finely chopped flat-leaf parsley

¼ cup tahini

1 Tbsp lemon juice (1 medium lemon)

½ tsp Tabasco sauce

1 Tbsp salt

Makes 2 cups

Soak the chickpeas in 3 cups of water overnight in the fridge.

The next day, drain the chickpeas and put them in a large, heavy-bottomed soup pot with 5 cups of fresh, cold water. Bring to a boil, then turn down the heat to a steady simmer, cover and cook until tender, about 1 ½ hours. Drain and set aside to cool.

While the chickpeas are cooking, prepare the sunchokes. Do not peel them but scrub the tubers well as they often have lots of dirt clinging to their skins. Chop the sunchokes roughly into 2-inch pieces.

Preheat the oven to 400°F.

Arrange the sunchoke pieces on a baking sheet and drizzle them with 2 Tbsp of the olive oil. Roast in the oven for 30 minutes or until tender throughout.

In a food processor, pulse the cooked sunchokes until they are the size of peas. Add the chickpeas and blend until smooth. Add the fresh garlic, roasted garlic, parsley, tahini, lemon juice and Tabasco. Add the remaining oil and salt, and process until smooth.

. . . .

COOK'S NOTE: *We serve this on Roti (page 146) cut into triangles or on crostini. It is also great with fresh vegetables, like carrots, celery, cucumbers or red bell peppers. I love a sandwich of hummus, tomato, cucumber and olives.*

Guacamole

Perfectly ripe avocados are essential for making this tasty little appetizer dip. It's healthy and satisfying, and a doggone civilized way to start any Tex-Mex meal, or to snack on when margarita hour arrives. This dip is rich and creamy, but without bad fat. Avocados are so healthy you just feel good eating them! I call them "nature's butter."

2 ripe Haas avocados

1 Tbsp lime juice (1 medium lime)

1 tsp salt

1 plum tomato, seeded
and diced small

1 fresh serrano or jalapeño
pepper, seeded and diced small

½ white onion, diced small

⅓ cup chopped fresh cilantro leaves

Makes 2 cups

Mash the avocados in a bowl, drizzle in the lime juice and salt, then fold in the tomato, pepper, onion and cilantro.

Serve with fried tortilla chips or use as a side dish for Huevos Rancheros (page 49), or as a simple salad on a bed of finely shredded lettuce or cabbage.

. . . .

COOK'S NOTE: *Ripe avocado will have a little bit of give when pressed. Avoid overripe avocados as they'll be stringy and brown inside.*

Cajun Spiced Pecans

My parents lived on a pecan plantation outside Granbury, Texas, for 20 years, so I grew up with a surplus of these nuts. I've tried pecans what seems like a billion different ways, but this remains my all-time favorite.

2 Tbsp butter

3 cups pecan halves

½ cup packed light brown sugar

1 Tbsp ground cumin

2 tsp pure chili powder (make sure it's 100% chili)

1 tsp paprika

¼ cup apple cider vinegar

2 tsp salt

Makes 3 cups

Preheat the oven to 350°F. Line a baking sheet with parchment paper.

Melt the butter in a large frying pan over medium-high heat. Add the pecans and sauté for 3 to 4 minutes. Add the sugar and cook until lightly caramelized, about 4 minutes. Stir in the cumin, chili powder and paprika. Add the vinegar and cook until all the liquid evaporates, 3 to 5 minutes. Season with the salt.

Spread the pecans over the prepared baking sheet and bake for 3 minutes.

Allow to cool and crisp up for 20 minutes before eating. They can be stored for up to 1 week in a covered dish.

Broiled Olives

If you have never had a great olive, try shopping for them at a traditional Italian market or at Whole Foods (they often have a nice selection in the salad bar area). Since we have neither in Tofino, we rely instead on our friends Helen and Basil Koutalianos, who divide their time between Pitt Meadows, BC, and Greece. When they first heard I was putting their olives into a wood-fired oven they were not impressed, but after trying them they realized that the method brings out a special flavor. The aroma fills the dining room and prompts smiles all around.

1 cup Kalamata, Agrinion or Picholine olives (whatever your preference)

Makes 1 cup

Preheat the oven to 500°F.

In a steep-sided baking dish or pie pan, arrange the olives in a single layer and broil under high heat for 3 to 4 minutes, or until they are blistering and bubbling.

Serve warm fresh from the broiler on their own, or with sliced cheeses and meats.

Helen and Basil Koutalianos

PITT MEADOWS, BC

For nearly a decade, I've been sourcing organic olives and olive oil from Helen and Basil Koutalianos of Basil Olive Oil. They're a small mom-and-pop business, and I fell in love with their product after tasting it at the famous Bishop's restaurant in Vancouver. The olives they sell and use for their olive oil are grown at their single-estate family farm in Greece and imported to their processing facility in the Fraser Valley on BC's mainland. "Greece is blessed with a perfect climate and rich soil for the cultivation of olive trees," Basil says. "Truly the quality of its extra virgin olive oil has no equal. Greek olive oil is the link between God and man."

Helen has been dedicated to fine traditional foods all her life. "I remember sitting on my father's knee, eating fresh shrimp dressed with fresh lemon and olive oil,"

she says. "You have to do what you love and what you're passionate about. My husband and I are very happy knowing that the honesty of our harvest, and the freshness and quality we insist on, is something we can bring to Canada. Not everyone can be at the olive pressing, but we can bring the new harvest here."

Helen and Basil's products are 100% organic, and they're of the highest quality you could imagine. Some of the most respected chefs in our region use their oil olive—for example, David Hawksworth, James Walt and Robert Clark—so you know they're doing it right.

SoBo Margarita

Back in the day when we moved from the old gravel parking lot to the Botanical Gardens we had a liquor license for the first time in SoBo history. The space was compact and the staff minimal, so we didn't want a full bar. We decided to focus on an outstanding wine list and local beers. But when we wanted to expand on our list and add a cocktail or two, I wanted to make the most of my favorite liquor: tequila. A hand-squeezed lime margarita was our choice. The thirst-quenching 3-ounce alcoholic beverage would soon become a signature SoBo cocktail and it's infamous around these parts. It is not unusual for us to squeeze 100 pounds of limes a week. The important part of the recipe is the little key limes that are grown in Mexico. They have a lot more juice than the larger Persian variety, and they just taste better.

1 cup key lime juice (25–30 key limes)

½ cup orange juice (1–2 medium oranges)

8 oz tequila

4 oz Triple Sec

1 Tbsp agave syrup

Loads of ice

4 key limes, quartered

2 Tbsp kosher salt

Serves 4

In a blender, place the lime juice, orange juice, tequila, Triple Sec and agave syrup. Blend on high for 20 seconds until the mixture turns a little frothy.

Take 4 very large glasses and run the pulp side of a lime quarter around the rim of each glass, using a fresh quarter for each one. Pour the salt onto a small plate. Turn the glasses upside down one by one and place the rims directly onto the plate. The lime juice will help the salt stick to the rim of the glass.

Fill each glass with enough ice to reach the rim. Pour in the frothy mix and squeeze the juice from the remaining lime quarters on top.

SoBo Mains

Left Coast Seafood Stew 164

Spice-Crusted Mahi Mahi with Grilled Pineapple Salsa 166

Herb-Crusted Halibut with Lemon Vegetable Risotto 168

Roasted Halibut in Prosciutto with Romesco Sauce 170

Seared Wild Spring Salmon with Mushroom Ragù 174

Salmon with Sorrel Sauce and Layered Potatoes 177

Cedar-Planked Salmon with Warm Grains 178

Wild Spring Salmon Sushi Rolls 181

BBQ Pacific Octopus with Chinese Tomato Relish 185

Spot Prawns with Gnocchi and Carrot Orange Sauce 189

Seared Scallops with Sweet Pea Risotto Cakes 191

Beach Fire Crab 194

Summer Polenta Pomodoro with Fresh Pesto 196

Stuffed Similkameen Valley Chilies 199

Chicken Enchiladas 200

Smoked Turkey Breast with Sweet Corn, Chanterelles and Cipollini Onions 202

Maple Chili–Glazed Quail with Wild Rice Salad 204

BBQ Bison Flank Steak with Chimichurri Sauce 207

Braised Salt Spring Island Lamb Shanks with Shallot and Red Wine Sauce 209

Left Coast Seafood Stew

Just for fun we named this rich bouillabaisse after Tofino's left-leaning, free-thinking attitude. It's West Coast in all its bountiful glory. Don't like clams? No problem. You can mix and match the seafood to your own taste.

Broth

1 bulb fennel, white only, thinly sliced

2 Tbsp olive oil

2 leeks, whites only, thinly sliced

½ medium red onion, diced small

¼ cup minced garlic (10–12 cloves)

1 tsp saffron threads

2 cups small-diced tomatoes
(2–3 medium tomatoes)

½ cup dry white wine

4 cups Fish Stock (page 251)

Stew

6 medium red potatoes,
cut into 1-inch cubes

¼ cup butter

Salt and pepper

1 Tbsp olive oil, plus
extra for drizzling

Four 6 oz pieces halibut,
ling cod or combination

1 lb live mussels, scrubbed and
de-bearded (see sidebar)

1 lb live clams, scrubbed and
free of sand (see sidebar)

8 large raw shrimp or prawns,
peeled and deveined

¼ cup Red Pepper Aioli (page 165)

1 Dungeness crab, cleaned and
steamed for 12 minutes (see
sidebar page 194) (optional)

Serves 4

For the broth, in a medium saucepan over low heat, sauté the fennel in 2 Tbsp of the olive oil for 2 minutes. Add the leeks, red onion and garlic and sauté for another 3 to 4 minutes. Add the saffron threads and sauté for 2 minutes, then add the tomatoes, and sweat until all the vegetables are tender.

Turn up the heat to medium, add the white wine and reduce for 1 minute. Add the fish stock and simmer the broth uncovered for 20 minutes.

Preheat the oven to 375°F.

Place the potatoes in a small saucepan and add just enough cold water to cover them. Bring to a boil, turn down the heat and simmer uncovered for 5 minutes. You want the potatoes to just cook through, tender enough to be easily pierced by a fork but not mushy. Strain the potatoes and make sure they are as dry as possible before roasting.

Melt the butter in a small saucepan over low heat. Add the potatoes with salt and pepper to taste, and toss in the butter until coated. Place the potatoes on a baking sheet and bake in the center of the oven for 10 to 15 minutes, until they are golden brown, crispy croutons.

Meanwhile, lightly oil another baking sheet with the 1 Tbsp olive oil. Season both sides of the halibut and/or ling cod with salt and pepper. Place the fish on the baking sheet and drizzle a little more olive oil overtop. Bake the fish pieces for about 10 minutes or until opaque throughout (try to time this so the potatoes and fish finish at same time; the fish should be on a higher rack than the potatoes).

While the potatoes and fish are baking, increase the heat under the broth to high and add the mussels and clams to the pot. Cover and steam them for 1 to 2 minutes, then turn the heat down to medium and add the prawns for another 1 to 2 minutes. Discard any mussels or clams that do not open. The prawns should be pink but not overcooked.

Divide the baked fish pieces between four bowls. Ladle the shellfish and broth overtop. Top with crispy potato croutons and drizzle with red pepper aioli.

If you are using the crab, evenly divide the crabmeat between the bowls of stew once plated. For visual effect we lay a few of the legs and the claws on top. Serve with some crusty bread on the side for soaking up the leftover broth.

Red Pepper Aioli

1 egg yolk

½ cup puréed roasted red
pepper (page 252)

2 Tbsp lemon juice (1 medium lemon)

2 Tbsp white wine vinegar

4 tsp minced garlic (4–6 cloves)

1 tsp smoked paprika

1 cup olive oil

½ tsp salt

Makes 1 cup

In a food processor, combine the egg yolk, red pepper purée, lemon juice, vinegar, garlic and paprika. Pulse for 2 seconds then, with the motor running, drizzle the oil in slowly until the mixture becomes creamy. Add the salt to taste. Refrigerate the mixture for up to 2 to 3 days.

Prepping Shellfish

DE-BEARDING MUSSELS: Under running water, scrape the hairs off the outer shells. With a paring knife, delicately twist/cut off the hairy "beard" at the base of the mussel (don't pull so hard as to damage the interior mussel).

CLEANING CLAMS: Soak the clams in a bowl of cold water for 20 minutes. Lift them out by hand or with a slotted spoon so that whatever sand or sediment that was ejected by the live clams remains in the bowl.

Spice-Crusted Mahi Mahi
with Grilled Pineapple Salsa

When I started cooking professionally, I was in Florida, where mahi mahi is still often referred to as dolphin fish. This really freaked me out until I learned that mahi mahi wasn't the same as Flipper, the bottle-nosed dolphin on the TV show of the same name, which I had grown up with. Mahi mahi has light pink, toothsomely firm flesh with a delicate, sweet flavor. It really shines with the smoky, tangy pineapple salsa.

Grilled Pineapple Salsa (page 167)

2 Tbsp olive oil, plus extra
for oiling your grill

1 Tbsp kosher salt

2 tsp ground ginger

1 tsp ground cumin

1 tsp ground coriander

Pinch cayenne pepper

2 cups baby spinach leaves

2 cups arugula

Four 6 oz skinless pieces mahi mahi
(or any local white fish that is at least
½ inch thick, such as halibut or tuna)

¼ cup extra virgin olive oil

2 Tbsp lime juice (1 medium lime)

Serves 4

Prepare the grilled pineapple salsa and set aside.

Preheat the BBQ to high and lightly oil the grill with a little olive oil.

Toss the salt with the ginger, cumin, coriander and cayenne pepper in a bowl to make a spice rub. In another bowl, mix the spinach and arugula together and set aside.

Brush the fish lightly with the 2 Tbsp olive oil and sprinkle or gently pat the spice rub on one side of the fish only. Gently lay the fish on the grill, spice side down. Grill for 3 to 4 minutes on the first side, or until the fish releases easily from the grill. Turn the fish and grill for 2 to 3 minutes on the second side. Mahi mahi should be cooked until just flaky.

Drizzle the ¼ cup extra virgin olive oil and lime juice over the arugula and spinach right before serving. Lay a bed of salad on each plate, place the fish on top and garnish generously with salsa.

Grilling Fish

Be careful not to turn the fish too quickly or it will tear. Use a flat metal spatula for turning rather than tongs as they will damage the fish. Learning how to judge doneness with fish is a delicate art—20 to 30 seconds can make all the difference in the world, so watch carefully! If the grill is too hot, you will burn the outside of the fish before the inside is done.

Grilled Pineapple Salsa

You will need a grill pan or an actual grill for the pineapple in this salsa. It is the vital step in adding smokiness and depth to the star of this recipe. You could skip the grilling but that would give a different end result (not bad, but not as complex a flavor). A great substitute for pineapple could be peaches when they're in season, as they grill really nicely. Play around with the spice levels of this salsa if you want, and change up the herbs as well. Cilantro or basil work well.

½ golden pineapple

2 Tbsp olive oil

1 red bell pepper, seeded and diced small

1 jalapeño pepper, seeded and minced

½ medium red onion, diced small

¼ cup minced fresh mint

¼ cup rice vinegar

Salt

Makes 3 cups

Preheat the BBQ to medium-high.

Wash and peel the pineapple, removing the prickly parts, then slice into ½-inch rounds. Brush the slices lightly with the olive oil and grill on the BBQ for 1 to 2 minutes per side, or until dark grill marks start to show. The pineapple should be caramelized but not mushy. Allow to cool for a few minutes and then dice it into small chunks, discarding the tough core.

In a medium-sized bowl, lightly toss the pineapple with the bell pepper, jalapeño, red onion, mint and rice vinegar. Salt to taste.

Herb-Crusted Halibut
with Lemon Vegetable Risotto

Halibut fishing usually starts around the middle of April here on the West Coast. It's one of the first signs of spring, followed by asparagus, then morels and peas. By this time of year we've all grown tired of root vegetables and our systems and senses need a wake-up call. This recipe is not complicated but it does require the finest-quality seasonal vegetables. I never give in to the supermarket selling asparagus from South America year-round. Enjoy it fresh for the eight weeks it's around and pickle some for later.

Lemon Risotto (page 216)

1 cup Vegetable Stock (page 250)

1 cup chopped flat-leaf parsley

1 cup chopped fresh basil

2 Tbsp minced garlic (3–4 cloves)

¼ cup extra virgin olive oil

1 Tbsp lemon juice (1 medium lemon)

2 tsp salt

8 fresh morel mushrooms, cleaned free of dirt (see sidebar)

2 Tbsp salted butter

2 Tbsp olive oil

Four 6 oz halibut fillets

8 stalks asparagus, each cut into 4 pieces

½ cup fresh peas (frozen also work)

Serves 4

Prepare the lemon risotto and set it aside in its pan. Prepare or have ready the vegetable stock.

Preheat the oven to 400°F.

In a blender or food processor, pulse the parsley, basil and garlic with the ¼ cup extra virgin olive oil, lemon juice and 1 tsp of the salt to form an herb pesto. Set aside.

Slice the mushrooms into quarters or rings. Heat the butter in a small sauté pan over medium heat, and add the morels as soon as the butter melts. Cook for 3 to 4 minutes, tossing often. Season them with the remaining 1 tsp of salt as soon as they are removed from the heat.

Heat the 2 Tbsp olive oil in a large, heavy-bottomed ovenproof frying pan over high heat. When the pan is very hot, add the halibut. You should hear a sizzle when the fish is added. If you don't hear anything it means the pan is not hot enough, so turn up the heat if you can. Cook the fish in batches to avoid overcrowding the pan. Sear the fish for about 3 minutes, turning it when it releases easily from the frying pan. Spread over top each fish piece one-quarter of the herb pesto, then place the frying pan in the oven for 4 to 5 minutes. The halibut should be moist and white in the center when it is ready. Halibut is known to dry out if overcooked so keep a watchful eye.

While the fish is in the oven, bring a large pot of water to a boil and blanch the asparagus and peas for 45 seconds. Drain and add the vegetables to the lemon risotto, then fold in the morels.

To serve, divide the risotto between four plates and place the herb-crusted halibut on top.

Cleaning Morels

The biggest challenge with morels is how to properly clean them without tearing them apart or soaking them in water. Morels have a lot of holes where dirt can hide. I start by tapping them lightly on a cutting board to loosen any dirt. Then I take a soft brush (either a new toothbrush or one of those mushroom brushes you can find at specialty cookware shops) and lightly brush each one. If they are really dirty I resort to quickly dunking them in cold water and drying them right away with paper towel or a clean kitchen cloth. Mushrooms have a high water content so adding more water doesn't do them any favors during the cooking process.

Roasted Halibut in Prosciutto
with Romesco Sauce

As soon as I arrived in Tofino I started cooking halibut this way, and it is now one of my go-to recipes. I have always been fond of the bold flavors of Spanish cuisine, and felt like the oh-so-mellow halibut could use a little jolt. Pork and fish go so well together, and the protective layer of prosciutto in this recipe helps maintain the moisture of the lean halibut.

1 cup Romesco Sauce (page 170)

16 small organic potatoes

6 Tbsp olive oil

16 stalks asparagus

Four 6–8 oz pieces halibut

Salt and pepper

4 large slices prosciutto

Serves 4

Prepare the romesco sauce.

Preheat the oven to 400°F.

Lightly toss the potatoes in 2 Tbsp of the olive oil. Place the potatoes on a baking sheet and bake for 10 to 12 minutes, or until tender. Toss the asparagus in another 2 Tbsp olive oil and roast asparagus on a separate baking sheet for 5 minutes.

Meanwhile, lightly season the halibut pieces with salt and pepper. Wrap 1 slice of prosciutto around each halibut piece.

In an ovenproof frying pan, heat 2 Tbsp olive oil over high heat until it starts to smoke. Lay the halibut in the oil very gently so as not to splatter. Cook the fish in batches to avoid overcrowding the pan. Sear the fish for 3 to 4 minutes then turn it over when it releases easily from the pan. Transfer the frying pan to the oven and bake for 3 to 4 minutes, depending on the thickness of the halibut, until it is white all the way through. It is crucial not to overcook the halibut as it dries out quickly and the prosciutto will get leathery.

Remove from the oven and place on a warmed plate. You can either top the fish with the romesco sauce, or plate the sauce first and lay it on top. A little romesco can go a long way when you're dealing with a delicate item like halibut, although I do love the sauce to spill over onto the potatoes and asparagus, too. Arrange the roasted vegetables around the fish and serve immediately.

Romesco Sauce

4 plum or Roma tomatoes

2 red bell peppers

1 cup almonds

4 cloves garlic, chopped

1 ½ slices day-old bread,
cut into 1 ½-inch cubes

¾ cup olive oil

½ cup red wine vinegar

2 tsp salt

½ tsp chili flakes

Makes 2 cups

Preheat the oven to 450°F or the BBQ to high.

Char the tomatoes and peppers until blackened, either on a baking sheet in the oven, or directly on the BBQ grill (see page 252). Set the tomatoes aside to cool enough for you to peel off the outer skins. Place the bell peppers in a bowl, tightly covered with plastic wrap, for 30 minutes. When they are cool, remove the skins by rubbing them off. Core and seed the peppers, and set aside.

Turn down the oven to 375°F.

Toast the almonds on a baking sheet for 5 minutes, allow them to cool for a couple of minutes, then pulse them in a food processor or blender until roughly chopped. Add the peeled tomatoes and peppers with the garlic, bread, oil, vinegar, salt and chili flakes. Blend until rough and rustic in consistency.

. . . .

COOK'S NOTE: *Romesco sauce is usually served at room temperature. It's a very quick and easy recipe that packs a lot of flavor, and it's great on vegetables. It will keep in the fridge for 3 days but is best used fresh.*

Fall

Fall is most Tofino locals' favorite season. Steam still rises from the beaches on every clear dawn and the intermittent rains aren't as ferocious as they will be come winter. The tourists have returned home and the days are still long and languid with plenty of good weather remaining. The surf is huge and consistent, and the road shoulders are a blur of fresh faces bicycling with surfboards balanced over handlebars. It's not unusual for us to serve whole tables of customers still wearing their wetsuits! It's now the locals' turn to relax. They take in some bear watching of their own as the salmon return to Thornton Creek to spawn, and turn to the local forests for chanterelles and pine mushrooms. The smell and smoke of beach fires hangs over the town, as long evenings—filled with the howling of wolves and lit up by massive moons—are spent enjoying fresh corn, fire-roasted squash, Dungeness crab and cedar plank salmon. It's an idyllic lull before the storms.

Seared Wild Spring Salmon
with Mushroom Ragù

Early spring in Tofino means the first of the year's commercial salmon fishing. There's just something about the time of year that excites me to my core. The salmon are feeding on herring, shrimp and squid, which makes for a deeper red flesh. A few varieties of salmon can be used in this recipe: chinook (otherwise known as spring or king salmon), coho and sockeye. While I adore chum for chowder and smoking, it doesn't work so well here.

For this recipe you should make the Meyer Lemon Butter a few hours ahead of time. You also need to prepare the favas before starting to cook.

Meyer Lemon Butter (page 175)

1 cup shelled fava beans (see sidebar)

¼ cup plus 2 Tbsp olive oil

Four 6–8 oz salmon fillets

2 tsp salt

2 Tbsp butter

5 morel mushrooms, cleaned free of dirt (see sidebar page 159)

1 medium shallot, minced

16 stalks asparagus, cut into 1-inch pieces

½ cup Vegetable Stock (page 250)

Serves 4

Prepare the Meyer lemon butter and refrigerate for a few hours. Blanch and shell the fava beans.

When you're ready to start cooking, preheat the oven to 400°F.

Heat the 2 Tbsp olive oil in a large, ovenproof frying pan over medium-high heat almost to the smoking point. Season the salmon fillets with salt, then carefully lay them in the frying pan, making sure to not overcrowd the pan or splash any of the oil (use two pans if need be). Cook for about 3 minutes on the first side, or until the fish releases easily from the pan. Turn it when it's golden brown. Transfer the frying pan to the oven and cook the salmon for 5 to 7 minutes, until just cooked through and pink in the center. If you like your salmon rare, reduce the cooking time to 4 minutes and there will still be some red in the center.

While the salmon is in the oven prepare the ragù. Heat the remaining ¼ cup olive oil with the butter in a large, heavy-bottomed frying pan over medium-high heat. Add the morels and shallot and toss for 4 to 5 minutes or until the morels are tender and getting golden, crunchy bits at the edges. Add the asparagus and fava beans, and toss for another minute or two before adding the vegetable stock. Cook for another 2 minutes, adding salt to taste.

To serve, ladle the ragù on a plate, top with a fillet of salmon and crown with a thick pat, about ½ Tbsp, of Meyer lemon butter. The butter will luxuriously coat the fish and heighten the flavor of the ragù.

Prepping Fava Beans

Fava beans are a three-part prep job: shelling them from their pods, blanching them, then shelling them from their skins. This can be confusing for people who have never worked with favas before. You can eat the second skin, but really, why would you want to? Favas are so much better when double-shucked! It may seem time-consuming but it's truly worth it. There is nothing quite like a fresh young fava bean. Canned just don't cut it.

First, shell all the favas from their pods and then blanch them for 3 minutes in boiling salted water. Strain and shock them in an ice bath for 5 minutes to keep them from overcooking. When they are cool enough to handle, make a slight cut with a paring knife and pop the tender bean out of its skin. When all the favas are out of their skins, take a bite to see how much longer they might need to cook. You want them tender, not mushy. If they are soft all the way through then they can only take a few more seconds of heat, so add them at the very last second when making the ragù; if they still have a little resistance, follow the ragù recipe as is.

Meyer Lemon Butter

½ cup salted butter,
room temperature

1 Tbsp chopped fresh sorrel

Zest and juice of 1 Meyer lemon

Makes ½ cup

In a food processor or mixer, blend the butter until creamy. Add the sorrel, zest and juice and pulse briefly until incorporated. Lay the butter out on a piece of plastic wrap and roll into a tube, like a cigar. Refrigerate it until set, at least a few hours.

Simply slice off what butter you need, when you need it. It's called a compound butter and it's also delicious on steaks. Refrigerate for up to 2 weeks or freeze for up to 6 months.

Salmon
with Sorrel Sauce and Layered Potatoes

This dish is something that was never intended for the book. We had some leftover food during one of our photo sessions at the beautiful, rustic and remote Wickaninnish Island. As we needed to feed three families with kids while shooting photos for the book, some dishes just evolved into family meals. That's what happened here with a few potatoes, a bunch of sorrel and the mighty salmon! It was delicious, and after looking at the day's shots, we all agreed: who wouldn't want to cook this as a family meal?

Layered Potatoes (page 218)

2 cups fresh sorrel

½ cup whipping cream

2 Tbsp puréed Roasted
Garlic (page 252)

2 medium shallots, minced

1 Tbsp lemon juice (1 medium lemon)

1 tsp Tabasco sauce

½ tsp salt plus more to taste

2 Tbsp canola oil

Four 6–8 oz salmon fillets,
boneless and skinless

1 lemon, sliced into 4 equal rounds

¼ cup olive oil

2–3 cups Swiss chard, stems
removed (about 6–8 large leaves)

Serves 4

Prepare the layered potatoes.

Preheat the oven to 375°F.

In a blender or food processor, place the sorrel, cream, roasted garlic, shallots, lemon juice, Tabasco and salt, and pulse until smooth.

Add the mixture to a small saucepan and heat over medium heat for 4 to 5 minutes, whisking frequently (if you like a thicker sauce, keep whisking, and allow the cream to reduce for an additional 5 minutes).

Heat the canola oil in a large, ovenproof frying pan over medium-high heat. Season the fish with a little salt and place it in the hot pan. When the fish releases easily from the frying pan, about 2 minutes, carefully turn it over. Top each piece of salmon with a lemon round and transfer the frying pan to the oven for 4 to 6 minutes to finish cooking. The time will vary depending on thickness of the salmon. Keep in mind that salmon cooks quickly and is best not overcooked.

Heat the olive oil in a medium-sized sauté pan over high heat. Add the Swiss chard and use tongs to stir it delicately. The greens will start to shrink down rapidly and will take about 4 minutes to cook.

To serve, place the wilted Swiss chard in the center of each plate. Place a portion of layered potato on the chard, ladle ½ cup sorrel sauce over each portion and place a salmon piece with a lemon round on top over the sauce.

. . . .

COOK'S NOTE: *If you can't source Swiss chard, try spinach, which only takes about 2 minutes to wilt. Sturdier greens, such as kale, usually take a little longer. Personally, I love mustard and collard greens, but often find that people just don't cook them long enough.*

Cedar-Planked Salmon
with Warm Grains

Nothing says West Coast like a piece of fresh salmon cooked on cedar. I use two methods for cedar planking. If I am cooking on the BBQ, I like to leave the salmon as one full side and use one cedar plank big enough to lay it out. If I am cooking in the oven, I prefer to pre-portion the salmon and cook on smaller, individual planks, to give me more flexibility with oven space. This recipe is fairly quick and easy, and is delicious served on top of the Warm Grains.

Warm Grains (page 217)

1 large or six small untreated cedar plank(s)

1 cup packed brown sugar

¼ cup dry mustard

2 tsp salt

½ cup olive oil

1 side salmon (2–3 lb) or six 8 oz salmon fillets (chinook, coho and sockeye are my favorite varieties for planking)

Serves 6

Prepare the warm grains and keep warm.

Preheat the oven to 450°F. Or, if cooking outdoors on a BBQ, preheat the grill to medium-high.

Mix the brown sugar with the dry mustard and salt to create a dry rub for the fish. Rub the olive oil on both sides of the fish and coat the top side with the dry rub.

Place the fish on the cedar plank(s) and roast in the oven for 8 to 12 minutes (depending on the thickness of the fish), or until just cooked through. If you are using a BBQ, the cooking will take roughly 20 minutes. Be sure to close the lid on the BBQ and check on the fish every few minutes.

These days a lot of people enjoy their salmon medium-rare. I like mine medium to well done, or until there is just a small line in the middle that is still red. That being said, undercooked salmon is better than overcooked salmon, so always err on the side of caution.

Cedar Planks

We get our cedar planks from our friend Steve on Wick Island, but I understand that not everyone has their own Steve. Source yours at your local hardware store and make certain that the wood is untreated. Untreated means no chemical compounds are in the wood, which is crucial as these can be toxic. I recommend using cedar shingles or even cedar fence wood. There are special cedar planks available at gourmet stores, but they're expensive and no better than anything you'd find at a regular hardware or grocery store. If you are using a direct flame—BBQ or open fire pit—soak the planks in water for a few hours before using them. If you are using your oven, keep them dry.

Wild Spring Salmon Sushi Rolls

I love sushi of all types, shapes and sizes. When I was asked to create a few salmon dishes for a TV show about a decade ago called *Hook, Line and Supper,* I needed to come up with something that the very serious and experienced salmon fisherman who hosted had not tried before. So that he would actually try the food, I could think different but not too far outside the box. He was not impressed when I said I was doing sushi, but the salmon inside the roll was a perfect medium-rare and the sea lettuce was so fresh and vibrant, he absolutely loved it!

½ cup sesame seeds

Sushi Rice (page 182)

1 carrot, julienned

1 cucumber, julienned

1 red bell pepper, julienned

8 sheets nori (dried seaweed sheets)

¼ cup wasabi paste

1 ½ cups fresh sea lettuce, chopped (if sea lettuce is not available, a fresh, crunchy leaf lettuce will also work)

2 lb wild spring salmon, cut into eight 4-inch-long strips

2 egg whites

½ cup Panko breadcrumbs

¼ cup canola oil

2 Tbsp sesame oil

¼ cup soy sauce

Makes 8 rolls (serves 4, or 8 for appetizers)

. . . .

COOK'S NOTE: *You can roll all the sushi in advance and keep it in the fridge, searing the rolls right before serving, as they benefit from the last-minute hot/cool contrast. These rolls are excellent with Seaweed Salad (page 102).*

Preheat the oven to 325°F. Spread the sesame seeds on a baking sheet and toast for 3 minutes. Remove from the oven and set aside to cool.

Prepare the sushi rice.

Mix the julienned vegetables together, then divide into eight small portions and set aside.

Place one sheet of nori, shiny side down, on a bamboo sushi-rolling mat. Spread one-eighth of the rice evenly on the nori. Spread a thin layer of wasabi (about 1 tsp) down the center of the rice. Top with one-eighth of the sea lettuce, one-eighth of the vegetable mixture and one strip of salmon. Roll the sushi into a cylinder. Press the mat around the roll to seal the edges. Repeat this process until all eight rolls are complete.

In a small bowl, whip the egg whites until light and fluffy, about 2 minutes. Pour them into a pie pan. In a second pie pan or on a plate, combine the Panko and sesame seeds. Lightly dip and coat each roll in the egg whites, then dredge in the Panko mixture to coat evenly.

Heat the oils together in an ovenproof frying pan over medium heat and sauté the rolls, turning on all sides until they are evenly browned, about 4 minutes. The salmon will be rare to medium-rare. If you want it cooked through, transfer the rolls to a pan and cook in a preheated 400°F oven for 3 to 4 minutes.

Remove the rolls from the frying pan (or oven), and slice into six ½-inch-thick pieces. Serve with the remaining wasabi paste and the soy sauce on the side.

continued on next page

Sushi Rice

Sushi is one of our family's favorite things to eat, and it's a wonderful way to showcase the premium seafood of the Pacific Northwest. This rice recipe is mostly foolproof if you measure correctly, and a good wooden bowl and paddle also help. A rice cooker is an excellent investment if you are a sushi fan.

4 cups uncooked sushi rice

2 Tbsp sugar

1 Tbsp salt

¼ cup rice vinegar

Makes enough for 8 sushi rolls or 20 tofu pockets

Place the rice in a fine mesh sieve and rinse under cool running water to get rid of excess starch. Rinse until the water runs clear, about 5 minutes, rubbing the rice between your palms to speed things up. Drain off the excess water and let the rice rest for 30 minutes in the sieve.

In a rice cooker, add the rice with 3 cups cold water to fill the cooker up to the 4-cup mark. Start the rice cooker. If you are cooking the rice on the stovetop, combine the rice and cold water in a covered medium-sized pot and bring to a boil. Turn the heat to low and simmer, still covered, for 20 minutes. Once the rice is done, remove it from the heat and let it rest for 30 minutes with the lid still on.

While the rice is cooking, place the sugar and salt in a small saucepan over low heat and dissolve them in the vinegar. This will take about 3 minutes. Stir and set aside until needed.

Transfer the cooked rice to a large wooden or plastic bowl. Cool it by constantly fanning and slicing through it with a flat paddle or wooden spoon. The object is to cool the rice quickly and separate the individual grains. This process should take about 10 minutes. If you paddle too much, though, the rice will be gummy. Season the rice with the vinegar mixture, while continuing to fold and fan. Add a little at a time until all the vinegar mixture has been absorbed.

Once the rice is cool, cover it with a damp towel and let it rest for 10 minutes.

Doug Kimoto
UCLUELET, BC

Doug Kimoto is a third-generation salmon fisherman who has been selling us spring salmon for the past few years. Following a long and proud family tradition, he fishes from *La Perouse*, a 42-foot troller that his father bought in 1950.

These days, there aren't many people who fish with the integrity Doug does. Salmon is the lifeblood of the West Coast, and respect for this resource is key for him. The quality of his fish is beyond anything I've ever seen—trust me, I've bought boatloads. He's campaigned for the local commercial industry for years and follows the guidelines of a sustainable fishery even in times of economic strife. He's also been involved in new fish-tracking systems that will allow consumers to find out exactly where their fish was caught, helping to raise the public's knowledge of what's on their plate. Doug works with honor, and he always shows up at our back door with what I can confidently say is some of the most beautiful salmon in the world.

"It's my love of fishing that drives me to keep doing it," he says. "And I get to see my connection to people's food experience in a restaurant—that's why I take pride in delivering a prime-quality product to the chef."

BBQ Pacific Octopus
with Chinese Tomato Relish

It was tough when the SoBo food truck expanded to include an evening dining room in Tofino's Botanical Gardens. We needed to hire a few new cooks as I needed to be home with three-year-old Barkley. I was also very pregnant with Ella, so shorter days were part of my reality. I hired a couple of surfer dudes—an Aussie named Reese and a Kiwi named James—and tried to let go a little. They had a big hand in creating this particular recipe. The ginger and tomato are just beautiful together, and the pickled cucumber adds just the right final hit of acid to tickle and refresh the palate. (Note that this dish needs to marinate for at least 24 hours.)

1 whole Pacific octopus (about 2 ½ lb)

1 large yellow onion, left whole

2 Tbsp salt

2 bay leaves

1 lemon, halved

2 bunches cilantro

1 bunch flat-leaf parsley

1 tsp ground cumin

½ tsp ground coriander

3 cloves garlic

2-inch piece fresh ginger, chopped

¼ cup lime juice (2 medium limes)

¼ cup olive oil

1 tsp sambal oelek (or chili garlic sauce)

Pickled Cucumbers (page 186)

Chinese Tomato Relish (page 186)

Serves 8

Place the whole octopus, onion, salt, bay leaves and half the lemon in a large stockpot with 6 quarts of cold water (see sidebar page 186). Bring to a boil then reduce the heat and slowly simmer uncovered for 1 ½ to 2 hours. When the onion is tender throughout, the octopus is usually ready. You can also check by slicing a piece off the thick end of a leg and having a nibble. If it's good and tender, it's ready!

While the octopus is cooking, prepare the marinade. Blend the cilantro, parsley, cumin and coriander with the garlic, ginger, lime juice, olive oil and sambal oelek in a food processor until it forms a paste (or finely chop the herbs, garlic and ginger and mix well with the spices, lime juice, oil and sambal oelek). Transfer to a very large bowl and set aside.

When the octopus is ready, remove from the heat and drain. Cut the legs from the body and slice them into 4- to 6-inch pieces. (The top part of the octopus, or the "cape," is edible but is not as tender as the legs, so I discard it at this point.) Place the octopus pieces immediately (while still hot) in the marinade. Allow the octopus to cool to room temperature, about 1 hour, then cover the bowl and refrigerate for at least 24 hours, but no longer than 48, to fully marinate.

About 2 hours before grilling the octopus, prepare the pickled cucumbers and the tomato relish.

Preheat the BBQ to high and lightly oil the grill.

Grill the octopus to warm it throughout and get grill marks, 4 to 5 minutes, turning frequently so as not to burn. You can get similar results in a preheated 500°F oven, turning once.

Serve the octopus on top of the tomato relish and garnish with a few pickled cucumber slices.

continued on next page

Pickled Cucumbers

1 ½ cups apple cider vinegar

½ cup sugar

1 cucumber, unpeeled

12–16 slices

In a small saucepan bring the vinegar and sugar to a boil. Remove from the heat and let the mixture stand to cool. Slice the cucumber lengthwise, as thinly as possible, either by hand or using a mandolin. Place the slices in the vinegar-sugar solution for 15 to 20 minutes. Strain through a fine mesh sieve and refrigerate for at least 1 hour before serving. The cucumbers will last for up to 3 days in the fridge but are best fresh.

Chinese Tomato Relish

¼ cup canola oil

1 large red bell pepper, cut into ¼-inch pieces

1 small red onion, chopped

½ cup chopped garlic (2–2 ½ heads)

4-inch piece fresh ginger, chopped

3 medium tomatoes, chopped

¼ cup fish sauce

¼ cup honey

2 Tbsp lime juice (1 medium lime)

1 small bunch cilantro, chopped

Makes 3 cups

Heat the oil in a heavy-bottomed sauté pan over medium heat. Sweat the peppers, onion, garlic and ginger until translucent. Add the tomatoes and fish sauce. Bring to a boil and simmer uncovered for 15 minutes.

Remove from the heat and stir in the honey and lime juice immediately. Add the cilantro just before serving. This keeps in the fridge for 3 to 4 days but is best fresh.

Laura Neufeld
UCLUELET, BC

Laura is a prawn fisherwoman who's been working the waters of BC for the last 20 years. Commercial fishing is still a male-dominated arena, but this gal certainly holds her own. And the spot prawns she brings in are divine.

The best thing in the world really is a tasty, fresh-out-of-the-water prawn—just *heaven*. If the only prawns you've ever eaten are the huge frozen ones you get in chain stores, you haven't really lived. BC's spot prawns are caught wild in the spring months, and they are a true delicacy that not many people know about. They have been mostly shipped direct to Asia through the last decade, as the Japanese and Chinese markets put a high value on them. But times are changing, and Laura is the kind of person who thinks of her community first. She has worked hard to be able to sell her product at a reasonable price here at home, and we now buy about 1,000 pounds of prawns from her every year. Her boat is so tight and clean you could literally eat off the deck—and I guess we kind of do, since the huge traps are all unloaded there!

You don't see the long hours of hauling gear in cold rain and choppy seas that go into prawn fishing, so it's worth remembering the work of people like Laura the next time you whip up a plate of spot prawns.

Spot Prawns
with Gnocchi and Carrot Orange Sauce

I love this dish! The luxurious sauce, developed in collaboration with my sous chef at the time, Aaron Walsh, has been on our menu for over a decade. I used to do sea bass (it was the '90s!) with a sauce of carrot juice, ginger, curry leaves, lemongrass and coconut milk. It was delicious, but the sauce would always separate. Aaron came to me one day and said, "Let's keep the premise but replace the coconut milk with butter and cream so it's a more elegant sauce." Genius! It's been the same ever since, with gnocchi as its dance partner.

Carrot and Orange Sauce

4 cups carrot juice

1 ½ cups orange juice

⅓ cup white wine vinegar

⅓ cup dry white wine

¾ cup whipping cream

6 Tbsp cold butter, cut
into small cubes

Gnocchi

5–6 medium russet potatoes

1 cup flour

2 egg yolks, lightly beaten

2 Tbsp salt

1 Tbsp olive oil

Prawns

3 Tbsp olive oil

24 spot prawns, peeled and deveined

Salt

Wilted Spinach

3 Tbsp olive oil

1 lb spinach

2 tsp minced shallots (½ large shallot)

½ tsp salt

Serves 4–6

In this recipe everything except the sauce is sautéed almost simultaneously at the end, and it all comes together very quickly. I tackle it by preparing the sauce and gnocchi ahead of time (sometimes earlier in the day), then, when I'm ready to serve, reheating the sauce and sautéing the gnocchi, prawns and spinach at the last minute.

Sauce
Combine the carrot juice, orange juice, vinegar and white wine in a large, heavy-bottomed saucepan. You will need enough room in the pan for the mixture to get foamy as it heats and the volume to double. Bring to a boil, uncovered, over high heat. Turn down the heat to medium-low and simmer uncovered, whisking occasionally, until it has reduced to about 2 cups. This will take at least 30 minutes. The idea is to remove all the extra water from the juices.

In a separate pot, bring the cream just barely to a boil over medium-high heat. Turn down the heat to low and simmer uncovered until it has reduced by half. This should take about 10 minutes. Whisk the warm cream into the carrot reduction over low heat. Very slowly add the cold butter, a few cubes at a time to let the sauce emulsify, whisking as you add.

Set aside the sauce until you are ready to serve; you should refrigerate it if this will be longer than 2 hours. When you are ready to serve, warm the sauce slowly over low heat, while you finish the gnocchi and prepare the prawns and wilted spinach

Gnocchi
Preheat the oven to 400°F.

Bake the potatoes, uncovered, for 45 minutes or until soft all the way through. Remove from the oven and set aside until they are cool enough to handle.

continued on next page

COOK'S NOTE: *Freshly squeezed carrot juice is great but there are also good bottled carrot juices on the market. I like Boathouse or Naked Juice. This recipe calls for spot prawns, but halibut, lingcod or even chicken work equally well.*

Fill a large stock pot with very heavily salted water and bring it to a boil. Lightly oil a large baking sheet.

Scoop the potato flesh out of the potato skins and put it through a ricer or food mill. You can mash by hand if you prefer but the potatoes will not be as light and fluffy. Transfer to a large mixing bowl.

Make a well in the potatoes and add half the flour and the egg yolks. Using a dough scraper (or the back of a knife) cut the flour and egg yolks into the potatoes until all the flour has been incorporated. Work quickly but gently to keep the potatoes warm and pliable. If the dough remains sticky, incorporate more flour, a little at a time, until it is the consistency to roll out smoothly. Stop adding flour before the dough becomes dry or flaky.

Using your hands, form the potato dough into a ball. Knead it a few times, then roll it into a rope about ¾-inch wide. Cut the dough into pieces about 1 inch long.

Working in batches, put the gnocchi into the boiling water for about a minute, until they float. Using a slotted spoon, remove them from the water and set on the prepared baking sheet to cool. Repeat with the remaining gnocchi. Set aside the gnocchi until you are ready to serve.

When ready to serve, heat a frying pan over medium-high heat, add 1 Tbsp olive oil. Gently add enough gnocchi to fill about half the pan. It's important to heat your pan enough and to avoid overcrowding it. Otherwise you will end up with mushy potato dumplings instead of light fluffy gnocchi.

Toss the gnocchi frequently and cook until hot throughout and lightly golden brown. Repeat with the remaining gnocchi. Keep the gnocchi warm while you prepare the prawns and wilted spinach.

Prawns

Heat a heavy-bottomed frying pan over high heat and add 1 Tbsp of the olive oil. Working in batches, gently place the prawns in the hot pan, being careful not to overcrowd it. Season with salt to taste and sear for 30 seconds on each side or until pink and white. Do not overcook! Add more olive oil as needed to cook the remaining prawns.

Wilted Spinach

In a heavy-bottomed frying pan, heat the olive oil to the smoking point. Add the spinach all at once and start to toss immediately with tongs. Add the shallots and salt. The spinach will wilt very quickly, about 2 minutes. Remove from the heat and be ready to serve immediately.

Toss the gnocchi gently with the warm sauce and the prawns. Serve with the wilted spinach on top.

Seared Scallops
with Sweet Pea Risotto Cakes

This recipe came out of a brainstorming session a few years back, sitting around a table at SoBo with my then sous chef Aaron Walsh and a few junior cooks. We really wanted to use Qualicum scallops to create something fresh with zing that really spoke of late spring and early summer.

This recipe has a lot of steps but is totally worth the effort. Everything can be done in advance, so if you're entertaining, you can relax with your guests until 5 or 10 minutes before serving. Just heat up the pre-seared risotto cake in the oven at 350°F for 5 minutes and then sear the scallops. I like to serve these on plain white plates so the vibrant mint drizzle and watercress pop out at you.

Sweet Pea Risotto Cakes (page 192)

Lemon Mint Drizzle (page 192)

¼ cup olive oil

12–16 large sea scallops

1 tsp salt

½ cup fromage frais (see Cook's Note)

1 cup watercress

Serves 4

Prepare the risotto cakes and lemon mint drizzle. Keep the cakes warm in the oven while you cook the scallops.

Heat the olive oil in a nonstick frying pan over high heat.

Lightly season the scallops with the salt and place them flat side down in the hot frying pan. They'll cook quickly, so when they release easily from the bottom of the frying pan, 1 to 2 minutes, turn them over and cook the other side for only another 30 to 60 seconds. The scallops should be caramel brown on the outside, and tender and juicy, with a little white translucence remaining, on the inside.

To serve, spoon 2 Tbsp of lemon mint drizzle in the middle of each plate. Place a warm risotto cake on top of this puddle. Place 2 Tbsp fromage frais on top of each risotto cake and submerge a portion of watercress into the soft cheese (like a tree in a snow drift). Arrange three or four cooked scallops around plate. Drizzle the remaining dressing around the scallops.

....

COOK'S NOTE: *Little Qualicum Cheeseworks on Vancouver Island creates a fantastic fromage frais (aka fresh cheese) that we use in this recipe as a garnish. It's so creamy and delicious, bordering on the sweet, like a mascarpone that has been whipped to perfection. You should be able to find it at most specialty markets, and any cheesemonger worth their weight in curds will sell it.*

continued on next page

Sweet Pea Risotto Cakes

4 cups Vegetable Stock (page 250)

¼ cup olive oil

1 cup uncooked arborio rice

2 medium shallots, minced

1 Tbsp minced garlic (3–4 cloves)

½ cup dry white wine

1 cup frozen peas, thawed
and slightly mashed

¼ cup fresh mint chiffonade

¼ cup butter

¼ cup grated Pecorino cheese

2 eggs, whisked

1 cup dried breadcrumbs

¼ cup canola oil

Serves 4, or 8 as appetizers

In a saucepan over medium heat, bring the vegetable stock to a boil and keep it at a simmer.

Heat the olive oil in a heavy-bottomed pan over medium-high heat to just before smoking point. Add the rice and gently stir with a wooden spoon. Add the shallot and garlic and stir for a few minutes more to toast the rice.

When the rice starts to turn golden brown, add a splash of wine to test the temperature. If the temperature is right you will see the wine dance and sizzle. When it does, add the remainder of the wine. The rice will immediately start to absorb the wine. Before all the wine has evaporated, add 1 cup hot vegetable stock, stirring continuously. Start a slow, rhythmic pattern of adding 1 cup stock right before the last addition has evaporated. The rice will take about 20 minutes to get to the desired *al dente* stage. You may or may not use all of the stock; don't worry if you have a ½ cup or so left over.

When the rice is *al dente* add the peas, mint, butter and cheese, and stir to combine. Pour the risotto mixture onto a baking sheet to cool for at least 1 hour.

When the risotto has cooled enough to handle, roll it into balls the size of golf balls, then flatten into 3-inch-wide disks.

In a small bowl, place the whisked eggs, and in another small bowl place the breadcrumbs. Dip each cake in egg and then coat in breadcrumbs.

Heat the canola oil in a small sauté pan over medium heat. When the oil is hot, carefully add the risotto cakes in batches to avoid crowding the pan. Sauté the first side until golden brown, 2 minutes. Turn and cook on the second side for another 2 minutes, or until crispy.

Lemon Mint Drizzle

¼ cup finely chopped
fresh mint leaves

3 Tbsp Roasted Garlic
purée (page 252)

3 Tbsp balsamic vinegar

3 Tbsp lemon juice (1 medium lemon)

1 tsp lemon zest

¾ cup olive oil

Salt and pepper

In a bowl, combine the mint leaves with the garlic, vinegar and lemon juice and zest. Add the oil slowly, whisking until the dressing has emulsified.

Season to taste with salt and pepper. Refrigerate for up to 3 to 4 days, after which the mint will lose its vibrant green color.

Makes 1 cup

Beach Fire Crab

This cookbook came about through summertime crab boils, beach fires and friendship! We love the fun and action of tending the flames and picking the crab while kicking back with a cold beverage. One of my favorite things about this dinner is that clean-up is a breeze. Toss out the crab shells and what do you have? A pot, a few plates and maybe some cutlery (if the fancier folks used it), leaving you time for another beer!

One 4- × 4-inch piece kombu or dried kelp (optional, but ideal)

1 lemon, sliced

¼ cup salt

4 Dungeness crabs, whole, killed and cleaned (see sidebar)

1 red onion, sliced thinly

¼ cup extra virgin olive oil

¼ cup salt

2 Tbsp butter

Serves 4–6

Bring a large, heavy-bottomed stockpot with 8 cups of water, the kombu, lemon slices and salt to a full boil (the water should be like the ocean). Drop the prepped crabs into the pot and steam, covered, for 10 to 12 minutes. You want just enough water to cover the crab, and it will be almost completely evaporated when the crab is finished cooking. Check halfway through cooking to make sure your pot hasn't dried up.

If you can, serve the crab right away, as the meat pulls away from the shell more easily when warm. It is best served with Campsite Potatoes (page 219) and Fire-Roasted Corn (page 217). Prepare the potatoes right before boiling the crab; the corn will take about the same time as the crab to prepare.

If you're not serving the crab immediately, pull it out of the pot and plunge into cool water for a few minutes to stop the cooking process. Drain and keep refrigerated for up to 48 hours.

Prepping Crab

If your fishmonger is willing to kill and clean your crab for you, go ahead and let them do it—crabs can pinch the heck out of your fingers if given a chance! If you are faced with the task of killing it yourself, your main aim is to not get pinched first.

To kill the crab, some people like to use tongs to hold it down on a cutting board and then split it down the middle with a knife. My method is to rip off the back shell, which kills it instantly, but also leaves the crab whole for a nice, clean presentation. To do this, pick up the crab by its back claws and smack it down on the counter or the side of your sink to stun it. Then place it flat, hold down as many claws as you can on one side with one hand, and rip the shell off sideways from one side to the other (9 o'clock to 3 o'clock). It's difficult to describe, but there are lots of videos on YouTube where you can see it done.

To clean the crab, rinse off the brownish slime, the viscera, from the tops of the legs. Lastly, pluck off and discard the lungs; these are the inedible feathery underparts and will come off easily. The edible parts of the crab are the claws, legs and body.

Summer Polenta Pomodoro
with Fresh Pesto

This recipe was inspired by one of my first babysitters in Kansas City, a first generation Italian immigrant named Mary who almost never left her kitchen. She was like a second mother to me and I loved going to her house. She taught me so much about respecting ingredients and the traditions that surround them.

2 cups whole milk

1 Tbsp plus 2 tsp salt

1 cup coarse cornmeal

2 Tbsp cold butter, cubed

½ cup grated Asiago or Parmesan cheese

Pomodoro Sauce (page 149)

Herb Pesto (page 197)

1 Italian eggplant, sliced lengthwise about ½ inch thick

1 small zucchini, sliced lengthwise about ½ inch thick

1 small yellow squash, sliced lengthwise about ½ inch thick

1 red onion, sliced into rings

1 red bell pepper, seeded and quartered

½ cup olive oil

1 Tbsp canola oil

2 cups mixed greens

Serves 4–6

Preheat the oven to 300°F.

In a large ovenproof saucepan over medium heat, add the milk with 1 cup cold water and the 1 Tbsp salt. Cover and cook the mixture on the stovetop for 20 to 25 minutes, or until the milk is frothy like a latte. Keep a careful eye on it to avoid scalding the milk. Very slowly, add the cornmeal and whisk constantly until smooth. Place the lid back on the saucepan and put it into the oven for 20 minutes, stirring once after 10 minutes.

Once the polenta is out of the oven, stir in the butter with a wooden spoon, then the cheese. Quickly spread the polenta onto an 8- × 8-inch baking sheet and let it cool. Once cooled, place the polenta in the fridge to help it set, about 1 hour.

While the polenta is setting, prepare the pomodoro sauce and herb pesto. Set aside.

In a large bowl, toss the vegetables with the olive oil.

Soak a paper towel or cloth with the canola oil and use it to oil the BBQ grill, then preheat to medium-high. Lay the vegetables right on the rack and season them with the 2 tsp salt. Grill the vegetables until they have dark brown grill marks but are still slightly firm. This will only take a couple of minutes.

Once the polenta is set, cut it into six equal-sized pieces—triangles, rectangle or squares. Lightly oil the grill again, using the same cloth or paper towel. Lay the polenta directly on the grill rack and turn after about 3 minutes, or when you have well-defined grill marks, then grill for another 3 minutes on the second side.

To serve, lay the mixed greens in the center of each plate. Top with polenta and vegetables, then drizzle with spoonfuls of pomodoro sauce and herb pesto.

. . . .

COOK'S NOTE: *The pan you use for this recipe does not have to be 8 inches × 8 inches. It can be any size or shape you want as long as the polenta it produces is at least 1½–2 inches thick. If it's any thinner it won't hold up on the grill.*

Herb Pesto

We play around with the herbs and nuts in this recipe all the time. For pizza I like a more traditional basil taste; if I am adding it to a soup I might change the basil for spinach or watercress or mint.

½ cup pine nuts

1 cup fresh basil

1 cup flat-leaf parsley leaves

½ cup arugula leaves

½ cup grated Asiago or Parmesan cheese

Zest of 1 lemon

2 Tbsp lemon juice (1 medium lemon)

½ tsp chili flakes

½ cup extra virgin olive oil

1 tsp salt

Preheat the oven to 400°F.

Lay the pine nuts on a baking sheet and toast in the oven for 4 to 5 minutes, or until they start to smell like popcorn.

In a food processor or blender, combine the nuts, basil, parsley, arugula, cheese, lemon zest and juice, and chili flakes. Pulse 5 to 10 times, until the herbs are starting to break down. With the motor running, drizzle in the olive oil and blend until smooth. If you like your pesto thinner, add more oil. Add salt to taste at the end (the hard cheeses can vary in salt content so taste first). Refrigerate for up to 1 week, or freeze in ice cube trays for later use.

Makes 1 ½ cups

Stuffed Similkameen Valley Chilies

This is one of my all-time favorite dishes for the fall. It's my take on the classic *chiles rellenos* (stuffed chilies), with a much lower calorie count. I source my poblano chilies from my friends Art and Lina Nugteren, who have an organic farm near Cawston in the Okanagan Valley. They rolled up to the food truck seven years ago with a bunch of chilies, offering to sell me exactly what I'd been missing since I left Texas five years before. I couldn't help myself and bought everything they had in their car— probably 200 pounds of chilies!

1 medium sweet potato or yam, peeled and diced into 1-inch cubes

4 Tbsp canola oil

Salt

4 boneless and skinless chicken thighs

4 fresh poblano chilies, roasted (see page 252)

1 cup frozen corn kernels (or 2 ears of roasted corn, shucked, see page 253)

½ cup fresh cheese (queso fresco, feta or fromage frais)

4 Tbsp sour cream

4 sprigs fresh cilantro

Serves 4

Preheat the oven to 400°F.

Toss the sweet potato in 2 Tbsp of the oil and bake on a baking sheet for 30 minutes or until tender. Sprinkle with a pinch of salt and set aside. Keep the oven on.

Meanwhile preheat the BBQ to medium and lightly oil the grill. Salt the chicken. Grill the chicken for 4 minutes on each side or until cooked through. Allow it to cool for about 5 minutes then use your fingers to shred the meat.

Line a baking sheet with parchment paper.

In a large bowl, fold the shredded chicken with the sweet potato, corn and cheese. Divide the mixture into four equal portions and stuff a portion inside each roasted poblano, being careful not to tear them. The presentation is gorgeous when the chilies are kept intact.

Place the stuffed poblanos on the prepared baking sheet and bake in the oven for 12 minutes. Serve each chili topped with 1 Tbsp sour cream and a cilantro sprig.

. . . .

COOK'S NOTE: *While the chilies are great on their own, a side of rice and pinto beans (see page 213) finishes things off nicely. If you don't have a grill, then roasted, stewed or even pan-sautéed chicken is fine. The grill just gives that authentic Mexican flair to the dish. If you're vegetarian, this recipe works well with roasted mushrooms instead of chicken. Toasted pumpkin seeds are a nice addition as well.*

Chicken Enchiladas

For some reason, growing up in my parents' house meant chicken enchiladas every Christmas Eve. I have no idea how the tradition started, but writing the recipe down really makes me miss my dad. He loved Tex-Mex cooking as much as he loved watching me and my mom in the kitchen. He would tell us that we needed our own restaurant. We would just laugh and call him crazy. Why would we ever want to work that hard?

4 bone-in skinless chicken thighs

1 large white onion, diced

1 stalk celery, diced medium

1 cup chicken broth (leftover stewing liquid)

1 cup whipping cream

1 cup roasted and diced green chilies (see page 252)

1 cup sour cream

2 Tbsp lime juice (1 medium lime)

1 tsp salt

½ cup canola oil

Eight 6-inch corn tortillas

1 ½ cups shredded white cheddar or asadero cheese

Serves 4

. . . .

COOK'S NOTE: *You can make the sauce and get all the fillings ready in advance, but do not cover the tortillas with the sauce until right before baking them—otherwise you'll have soggy enchiladas! We love to serve our enchiladas with guacamole (page 156), pinto beans (page 213) and brown rice.*

Place the chicken, ½ cup of the onion and the celery in a medium-sized pot with 4 cups water and bring to a boil. Turn down the heat to low and gently simmer uncovered for about 15 minutes, or until the chicken is cooked.

Remove the chicken from the pot, leaving the stewing liquid in the pot. Let the chicken cool enough so that you can handle it, about 30 minutes, then shred it by hand, setting aside the bones. Set aside to cool for another 10 minutes then refrigerate. Place the bones in the stewing liquid and bring to a boil. Turn down the heat to low and simmer uncovered for 1 hour. Strain the resulting broth through a fine mesh sieve then put it back in the pot. Turn up the heat, and boil, uncovered, until it is reduced to 1 cup of liquid.

In a heavy-bottomed saucepan over medium-low heat, combine the chicken broth with the whipping cream and chilies and simmer gently uncovered for about 1 hour, or until the volume of the liquid has reduced by half, whisking often to prevent it from burning. Whisk in the sour cream, lime juice and salt to create a sauce.

Preheat the oven to 350°F.

Heat the oil in large frying pan over medium-high heat. Use tongs to dip both sides of each tortilla into the hot oil until just softened, about 5 seconds. Let any oil drip back into the frying pan and use paper towel to soak up any excess. Keep the tortillas covered so they don't dry out.

In a bowl, toss the chicken with the cheese and remaining ½ cup onion. Add about ⅓ cup of this filling to the center of each softened tortilla, then roll the tortilla up tightly like an open-ended burrito.

In a large ovenproof ceramic or glass baking dish, pour in enough sauce to coat the bottom of the dish. Lay the enchiladas side by side (not stacked), seam side down, and pour the remaining sauce overtop. Bake for 20 to 25 minutes, or until the sauce is bubbly and starting to brown on top.

Smoked Turkey Breast
with Sweet Corn, Chanterelles and Cipollini Onions

Fall seems to be the time of year when we start looking at turkey as more than just deli meat for sandwiches. This recipe is a comforting clash of Southern smoke and earthy mushroom, tied together with sweet corn. It's great for when you want to break away from the traditional turkey and trimmings. And it's a perfect meal for those fall days when the air is still warm from the disappearing summer, and the two seasons are one for a brief moment in time. (Note that this has to marinate for 12 to 24 hours, and requires a store-bought or homemade smoker—see sidebar.)

½ recipe Wet Brine (page 203)

1 ½ lb boneless turkey breast, skin on (about 1 breast)

2 cups alder, applewood or hickory chips

4 Tbsp olive oil

1 Tbsp salt

4 ears of corn

8 whole cipollini onions, peeled

¼ cup butter

1 lb chanterelle mushrooms, wiped clean of dirt and torn into bite-sized pieces

1 Tbsp finely chopped fresh sage

1 Tbsp finely chopped fresh flat-leaf parsley

Serves 4

Prepare the wet brine.

Place the turkey breasts and wet brine in a large stockpot (or any container big enough to hold them) and refrigerate for 12 to 24 hours.

Remove the turkey from the brine, pat it dry with paper towel and bring to room temperature before smoking. This usually takes about 1 hour, which is ample time to prepare the smoker.

If you have a store-bought smoker, follow its directions.

For homemade smokers (see sidebar), place the smoking chips in the large metal pan and add the wire rack. Heat the pan on the stovetop over high heat. The chips will start to burn. Place the smoker lid on top and allow the pan to fill with smoke for about 5 minutes. It's a good idea to ventilate your kitchen at this point to avoid your smoke detector going off.

Place the turkey directly on the wire rack. Turn down the heat to medium-high and cover with the smoker lid. Smoke the turkey until all the chips are burned up, about 25 minutes.

Preheat the oven to 400°F.

Rub the turkey with 2 Tbsp of the olive oil and the salt, place it on a baking sheet and roast for 10 minutes, or until cooked all the way through to an internal temperature of 165°F–170°F). Remove from the oven and allow to rest while preparing the sides.

Rub the corn ears with 1 Tbsp olive oil, place them on a baking sheet and roast for 20 minutes in the oven. Remove the corn from the oven and let it cool, then remove the kernels by running a sharp knife down the cob. Set aside.

In an ovenproof frying pan over high heat, add the remaining 1 Tbsp olive oil and the cipollini onions. Toss the onions to coat them well in the oil then transfer to the oven for 20 minutes, until tender and golden. Remove from the oven, set aside to cool then quarter.

Heat the butter in a large frying pan over medium-high heat. Add the mushrooms and sauté for about 5 minutes. Add the onions and corn and sauté for an additional 5 minutes or until the mushrooms are well cooked.

To serve, slice the turkey and divide it between four plates. Spoon the vegetables over top and sprinkle with the sage and parsley.

Wet Brine

A good poultry brine adds moisture to larger pieces of poultry or pork. You can store this brine in the fridge for up to 1 week. Juniper berries—about 1 Tbsp—make a fine addition to this brine at Thanksgiving.

12 cups water

1 cup salt

½ cup sugar

Makes enough for 1 whole turkey or 2 whole chickens

In a large stockpot, bring the water to a boil and add the salt and sugar, stirring to dissolve. Turn off the heat and let the brine cool.

Submerge the poultry in the brine. Cover and refrigerate for 24 hours.

Homemade Smoker

To make a homemade smoker, you need a large metal roasting pan, a wire rack and a lid (or aluminum foil). The pan should be something you can let get smoky and tarnished, so go for the garage sale special, but ensure that the wire rack fits inside and that it has a tight-fitting lid. If the lid is not tight, use aluminum foil instead.

Maple Chili–Glazed Quail
with Wild Rice Salad

The mild heat from the chili powder in this recipe teams up magically with the pure sweetness of the maple syrup. Use the freshest chili powder and highest grade of maple syrup you can find. I highly advise purchasing semi-boneless quail as you really want to eat quail with your fingers and the only bones you want to deal with are the little drumsticks. This recipe is so very finger-licking good!

Wild Rice and Dried Berry
Salad (page 94)

1 cup pure maple syrup (light or dark)

2 Tbsp chili powder

8 quail

2 Tbsp canola oil

2 tsp salt

Serves 4

Prepare the wild rice and dried berry salad.

Preheat the oven to 400°F. Preheat the BBQ to medium-high. Line a baking sheet with parchment paper.

Combine the maple syrup and chili powder in a medium-sized saucepan over low heat. The mixture will expand rapidly so you need extra space in the saucepan to start. Heat for about 5 minutes, whisk well and set aside.

Lightly coat the quail with the oil and salt. Grill the quail on the BBQ for 2 minutes on each side. Transfer them to the prepared baking sheet and pour the syrup over them. Finish in the oven for 2 to 3 minutes, until thoroughly cooked with an internal temperature of 145°F.

Serve two quail per person on a bed of the rice and berry salad.

BBQ Bison Flank Steak
with Chimichurri Sauce

Bison flank is a more economical cut of meat than beef tenderloin or ribeye steak, and it delivers just as much flavor as long as it's not overcooked or sliced incorrectly (see sidebar page 208). Bison is also usually grass-fed, so it has a more natural flavor.

2 lb bison flank, cleaned of any silver skin and cut into 4 steaks across the grain

Chimichurri Sauce (page 208)

1 ½ lb fingerling potatoes

4 tsp salt

1 lb green beans, stems trimmed

1 Tbsp canola oil

3 Tbsp olive oil

1 Tbsp butter

Serves 4

Bring the flank steaks to room temperature before grilling. This usually takes about 1 hour—just enough time to prepare the vegetables and sauce.

Prepare the chimichurri sauce.

In a heavy-bottomed saucepan, cover the potatoes with cold water and 1 tsp of the salt. Bring to a boil, turn the heat down and simmer for 10 minutes. Drain the potatoes and let them cool.

In a large, heavy-bottomed stockpot or saucepan, bring about 4 quarts of water to a boil (enough to cover the beans by 4–5 inches). Add 1 tsp of salt and blanch the beans for 3 to 4 minutes. Drain the beans and plunge them into an ice bath to stop the cooking process.

Soak a paper towel or cloth with the canola oil and use it to oil the BBQ, then preheat to high.

Rub the flank steaks lightly with 1 Tbsp of the olive oil (between all four) and some salt. Lay the meat directly on the grill rack and cook to a perfect medium-rare (see sidebar page 208). Remove from the grill and allow to rest, uncovered.

While the meat is resting, slice the potatoes in half lengthwise, rub with the remaining 2 Tbsp olive oil and place on the hot grill. After 2 minutes, the potatoes should be turning golden brown. Use a flat spatula to carefully turn the potatoes to finish on the second side for another 2 to 4 minutes, or until tender and golden. Salt to taste.

Right before serving, heat a large cast iron frying pan on the stovetop or BBQ. Melt the butter, then toss the green beans in the butter.

Slice each steak across the grain into 4 or 5 pieces, then fan out on each plate and spoon about ⅓ cup chimichurri sauce over top. Scatter the potatoes and beans around the plate, and either top with more sauce or serve it on the side.

continued on next page

Chimichurri Sauce

Chimichurri is to Argentina what salsa is to Mexico and what ketchup is to North America. It is a full-flavored herb sauce that isn't spicy. It pairs wonderfully with bison and is fresh and vibrant for the summer months. I like to prepare this sauce by hand and not in a food processor so that it keeps its rustic vibrance.

1 cup finely chopped flat-leaf parsley

½ cup finely chopped fresh oregano

¼ cup finely minced garlic
(10–12 cloves)

1 medium shallot, minced

¼ cup red wine vinegar

¼ cup lemon juice (1 large lemon)

¾ cup olive oil

Salt

Tabasco sauce (optional)

Makes 1 ½ cups

In a medium-sized bowl combine the parsley, oregano, garlic and shallots with the vinegar and lemon juice. Drizzle in the olive oil while whisking. Add salt and Tabasco to taste.

Grilling Flank Steaks

Flank steak is thin, about ¾ inch thick, so it cooks quicker than ribeye or chops. The rule of thumb for flank steak is to place it on the grill and leave it, untouched, for 3 minutes so that it can develop a crust. Then turn it over and grill for another 3 minutes for rare, or 4 minutes for medium-rare. Anything longer will give you a tough piece of meat. It's really important to allow the meat to rest for 5 minutes after it's been on the grill, and allow the juices to settle before slicing it. If you try to slice the flank in the same direction as the grain it will be very tough, so slice the flank across the very lean muscle fibers or across the grain.

Braised Salt Spring Island Lamb Shanks
with Shallot and Red Wine Sauce

This is a classic for the dead of winter when you're craving something rich, roasted and deeply satisfying. We're fortunate to be near Salt Spring Island, which has lovely lamb, so if you live in Canada try to find it. Otherwise, seek out a local farm that pasture-raised their lamb. Slow oven-roasting breaks down the tough gelatinous muscle so it becomes tender.

¼ cup canola oil

Four 1 lb lamb shanks

2 Tbsp plus 2 tsp salt, plus more to taste

¼ cup flour

2 onions, diced medium

8 cloves garlic, whole

4 carrots, each cut into 3–4 pieces

4 parsnips, each cut into 3–4 pieces

2 cups dry red wine

1 cup tomato paste

2 cups chicken, lamb or vegetable stock (see pages 250–51, or use store-bought)

4 bay leaves

4 sprigs fresh thyme

4 sprigs fresh flat-leaf parsley

Mashed Potatoes (page 219)

1 Tbsp olive oil

8 medium shallots, finely diced

Pepper

1 Tbsp chopped fresh flat-leaf parsley (optional)

Serves 4

Preheat the oven to 325°F.

Heat the oil in a heavy-bottomed, ovenproof frying pan over medium-high heat.

Season the shanks with the 2 tsp salt and dredge them in the flour. Sear them in the hot oil until golden brown on all sides, about 5 minutes in total. Remove the shanks from the pan, leaving the drippings behind.

Add the onions, garlic, carrots and parsnips to the pan drippings. Sauté for 2 minutes over medium heat. Add 1 cup of the red wine and the tomato paste. Cook for another 10 minutes, until all the wine has evaporated. Add the stock, bay leaves, thyme, parsley and the remaining 2 Tbsp salt. Bring to a boil and add the shanks back in.

Cover the frying pan tightly with aluminum foil and transfer to the oven to braise for 2 hours, or until the shanks are tender enough to be easily pierced by a fork. Remove from the oven and let cool. Separate the vegetables from the meat and set aside. Spoon out any excess fat from the juices. Keep 2 cups of the juices for the sauce.

Start to prepare the mashed potatoes as you make the red wine sauce.

Heat the olive oil in a medium-sized saucepan over medium heat and sauté the shallots for 4 to 5 minutes. Deglaze the pan with the remaining 1 cup red wine and cook for 5 more minutes, or until the volume is reduced by half. Whisk in the reserved braising juices. Season with salt and pepper to taste.

Serve the lamb shanks with the mashed potatoes and reserved vegetables. Pour ¼ cup sauce overtop each shank and garnish with fresh chopped parsley if desired.

. . . .

COOK'S NOTE: *You may choose to braise the lamb shanks the day before and reheat them before serving. Bring the meat to room temperature before reheating for best results. If you do it this way it's very easy to take the fat off the sauce.*

Sides

West Texas Onion Rings

Sweet, salty, sharp, tangy and crunchy—who can resist really good onion rings? This recipe was featured in the June 1999 issue of *Food and Wine* and the *Best American Recipes 2000* cookbook, edited by Fran McCullough and Suzanne Hamlin. It takes serious willpower to not eat these right out of the pan. Serve with my BBQ beef brisket sandwich (page 117) or veggie burger (page 120); or simply use them to top off a steak.

1 ½ cups buttermilk

1 ½ cups flour

2 Tbsp puréed canned chipotle chilies in adobo sauce

2 sweet onions, cut into ¼-inch-thick slices and separated into rings

1 ½ cups rice flour

1 ½ cups yellow cornmeal

1 Tbsp ground cumin

1 Tbsp cayenne pepper

4 cups vegetable or peanut oil, for frying

1 Tbsp salt

Makes 20–25 rings

In a large bowl, whisk the buttermilk with ½ cup of the flour and the chipotle chilies until smooth. Add the onion rings. Toss them to moisten then let them soak for 30 minutes.

In a separate bowl, combine the remaining 1 cup flour, rice flour, cornmeal, cumin and cayenne. Coat the onions in the spiced flour mixture, shaking off any excess.

Heat 2 ½ cups of the oil in a large cast iron frying pan to 350°F. Use a thermometer or test the heat with a bread cube—it should turn golden brown within 1 ½ minutes of hitting the oil. Fry the onion rings in batches, turning them often, until they are golden brown, 3 to 4 minutes. Add the remaining oil to the pan when it is empty (if needed) and heat to 350°F before continuing to fry the next batch of onion rings. Use tongs to transfer the onion rings to paper towel to soak up any excess oil. Season with salt and serve immediately.

. . . .

COOK'S NOTE: *The key to success with these addictive onion rings is to use sweet onions, such as Texas 1015s, or Walla Wallas from Washington State. Coat the onions in flour just before frying.*

Pinto Beans

At Cibolo Creek Ranch I had the pleasure of working with a very talented woman named Griselda Menchaca. She taught me a lot about proper Mexican cooking techniques. The first time she watched me cook beans she cocked her head to one side and said "no sé." She was asking me why I kept adding ingredients to the beans. I explained that the chilies, beer and stock I was putting in added flavor. Needless to say, she disagreed, and told me that adding other items to the beans often leads to toughness. She suggested we take a naked approach. I have followed her advice for the last 15 years and it has never let me down.

1 cup dried pinto beans

2 bay leaves

2 tsp salt

Makes 3 cups

Rinse the beans in a colander under cold water. Transfer them to a medium-sized soup pot, and add the bay leaves and 5 cups cold water. Bring to a boil, then turn down the heat to low and simmer, covered, for 2 hours or until the beans are tender. Check the water level after 1 hour and add more if needed. The beans will turn mushy and fall apart if you overcook them. You want them to be tender.

Remove from the heat and stir in the salt only *after* the beans are fully cooked. This is what Griselda was most firm on   if you add salt before the beans are fully cooked they will never become tender and will have a fibery toughness instead.

Allow the beans to cool completely (you can use the same method as chilling stock, see page 251) before refrigerating. They are good for about 4 days in the fridge.

. . . .

COOK'S NOTE: *I am surprised at how many folks do not cook their own beans but buy canned instead. It's a shame because you could not find an easier, less expensive or more nutritious food! You can use this recipe method to cook any type of dried beans.*

SoBo Slaw

This is my take on the old-school, creamy, sugary slaw that a lot of us grew up with. We love to add green papaya to this salad but it's hard to find where we are. Many vegetarians like it with stir-fried tofu and crushed peanuts on top. I like it on top of a piece of grilled halibut or tuna. It is also beautiful over green salad with avocado and orange slices, or with our Thai Chicken on Roti (page 145). Fresh herbs are essential.

Citrus Dressing (see below)

2 large carrots, julienned

1 medium jicama, peeled and julienned

1 red bell pepper, julienned

½ savoy cabbage, julienned

1 apple (Gala, Pink Lady or Granny Smith), julienned

1 cup combination of finely chopped fresh cilantro, basil and mint

Makes 6 cups

Prepare the citrus dressing.

In a large bowl toss the carrots, jicama, pepper and cabbage with the apple. Add the herbs and mix well.

Pour the citrus dressing over the slaw and mix well. This will stay lovely and crisp for 2 days in the fridge.

. . . .

COOK'S NOTE: *Play around with this recipe. If you're not keen on one of the herbs, fruits or vegetables listed, just substitute something else or leave it out. If you're not fond of cilantro, use more mint or basil. Slaw has no set rules; just make it fresh and do not hang onto it for more than a day or two.*

Citrus Dressing

1 cup orange juice

1 large shallot, minced

1 ½ Tbsp red wine vinegar

½ cup apple juice

2 Tbsp lime juice (1 medium lime)

1 Tbsp sambal oelek (or chili garlic sauce)

¼ cup canola oil

1 tsp salt

Makes 1 ½ cups

In a heavy saucepan over medium-low heat, reduce the orange juice by half. Remove from the heat and allow to cool. Combine the shallots and vinegar and set aside for 30 minutes. When ready, whisk the orange juice and vinegar mixture with the apple and lime juices, and the sambal oelek. Whisk in the oil, and season with the salt. Refrigerate for up to 4 to 5 days.

Lemon Risotto

I have three essentials for preparing this dish: a wooden spoon, a lot of love and a glass of wine.

¼ cup olive oil

1 cup arborio rice

2 medium shallots, minced

1 Tbsp minced garlic (3–4 cloves)

½ cup dry white wine

4 cups Vegetable Stock plus extra
½ cup if needed (page 250), kept hot

¼ cup lemon juice (1 large lemon)

¼ cup butter

¼ cup grated pecorino cheese

Serves 4

Heat the olive oil in a heavy-bottomed pan over medium-high heat. Add the rice and stir gently with a wooden spoon. Add the shallot and garlic and stir for a few minutes more to toast the rice.

When the rice starts to turn golden brown, add a splash of wine to test the temperature. If the temperature is right you will see the wine dance and sizzle. When it does, add the remainder of the wine. The rice will immediately start to absorb the wine.

Before all the wine has evaporated add 1 cup hot vegetable stock. Stirring constantly, add another 1 cup stock right before the last addition has evaporated until the stock has all been used up. It will take about 20 minutes for the rice to get to the *al dente* stage.

When the rice is *al dente*, add the lemon juice and stir to mix well. If you're serving the risotto right away, finish by adding the butter and cheese and gently stirring until both are melted. If you're not serving right away, reserve the butter and cheese, and pour the risotto onto a baking sheet to cool until needed. When you're ready to use the risotto, heat ½ cup vegetable stock in a medium-sized saucepan or frying pan over medium heat. When the stock is bubbling, add the cooked risotto and stir gently with a wooden spoon for about 5 minutes. Now add the butter and cheese and stir until melted.

. . . .

COOK'S NOTE: *Risotto should be creamy and loose on the plate, not in a clump. People often overcook the rice and do not add enough liquid. I never add the final butter or cheese until moments before serving.*

Warm Grains

This recipe uses both wild rice and quinoa, but feel free to choose just one of them if you'd prefer, or mix a few different grains together. This bed of grains works equally well with duck, chicken or a grilled Portobello mushroom cap.

½ cup Port Wine Vinaigrette
(page 92, but omit the oil)

1 cup uncooked wild rice

1 cup uncooked quinoa

½ medium red onion, diced

½ medium red bell pepper, diced

1 ½ cups de-stemmed
kale (or spinach)

Salt

Serves 6

Prepare the port wine vinaigrette, minus the oil.

Cook the grains according to the directions on their packages (cooking methods may vary).

Add the port vinaigrette to a large saucepan over medium-high heat. Add the onion, bell pepper then kale, and sauté for 4 to 5 minutes. Add the grains and mix to combine. Season to taste with salt.

Roasted Corn and Potato Hash

This hash is excellent for breakfast or brunch. It also goes well with Bennys (page 53) or with any other poached egg dish.

1 cup Fire-Roasted Corn (page 217), you can also use fresh or frozen and thawed kernels

4 medium Yukon Gold potatoes, skins on

½ cup canola oil

2 green onions, thinly sliced

1 tsp salt

1 tsp ground cumin

½ tsp smoked paprika

Serves 4

Prepare the fire-roasted corn.

In a large pot, cover the potatoes with cold water, then bring to a boil. Turn down the heat to low and simmer for 3 minutes. Drain and let them cool slightly before dicing into medium-sized pieces (ideally 1-inch cubes).

Heat the oil in a large, heavy-bottomed frying pan over high heat to the smoking point. Carefully add the potatoes, being careful not to splash the hot oil, and turn them to coat evenly in oil. Fry for 10 to 12 minutes or until lightly golden. Add the corn, onions, salt, cumin and paprika. Fry for another 3 minutes or until the potatoes are golden brown and tender enough to be easily pierced by a fork.

. . . .

COOK'S NOTE: *If you use frozen corn, be sure to thaw it thoroughly to cut down on the moisture.*

Layered Potatoes

The Layered Potatoes and the Mushroom and Potato Gratin (see the variation below) can both be made a day in advance. To reheat, cover and bake in a preheated oven at 350°F for 15 minutes. This will make the dish a little drier, which makes it easier to cut but less creamy.

4 Yukon Gold potatoes, scrubbed

1 Tbsp salt

1 tsp pepper

2 Tbsp butter

2 Tbsp whipping cream

Serves 4

Preheat the oven to 375°F. Lightly grease an 8- × 8-inch baking sheet or casserole dish with oil.

Slice the potatoes ultra-thin either by hand or with a mandolin. Place a layer of potatoes on the bottom of the prepared baking sheet. Season with a scant amount of salt and pepper and repeat the layering process until all the potatoes are gone, or the pan is three-quarters full. Halfway through, add a dollop of butter.

Drizzle the whipping cream over the top of the potatoes. Cover the pan with aluminum foil and bake for 30 minutes. Uncover and bake for another 20 minutes, or until the potatoes are tender enough to be cut with a fork.

Remove the potatoes from the oven and let cool for at least 30 minutes to set. Slice into squares and serve.

....

Variation: Mushroom and Potato Gratin
Serves 4

Preheat the oven to 400°F.

Thinly slice 20 de-stemmed shiitake mushrooms (to make ¾ cup), 1 large Portobello mushroom and 1 sweet yellow onion. Prepare 1 cup grated Swiss cheese.

Heat ¼ cup olive oil in a large frying pan over high heat, and sauté the mushrooms and onions with ¼ cup minced garlic for 10 minutes, or until tender. Set aside while you prepare the potatoes, as above.

When building the potato layers, alternate every layer of potato with a layer of the mushroom and onion mixture. Sprinkle cheese between each layer. Omit the butter and top with ½ cup whipping cream. Bake for 45 minutes.

....

Campsite Potatoes

The Restigouche River runs down the Quebec and New Brunswick border, and it's where Artie spent the majority of his childhood summers, camping and fishing. The grill was on for every meal, and this recipe was one of the weekly regulars prepared by his mom, Connie Ahier. It's still a camping staple with our clan, and pairs beautifully with a freshly caught salmon or trout.

2 lb red new potatoes, diced
into ½-inch cubes

1 medium onion, diced
into ½-inch cubes

1 Tbsp salt

1 tsp pepper

¼ cup olive oil

½ cup butter, cut into small cubes

Serves 4

Preheat the BBQ to high.

On an extra-large piece of aluminum foil, spread out the potatoes and onion. Season them with the salt and pepper, drizzle with the oil and scatter the cubes of butter overtop. Roll the foil up into a long cylinder-shaped bundle and twist the ends closed.

Place the foil bundle on the rack of your hot BBQ, turning every 10 minutes. This can become challenging if the aluminum foil starts to tear. If it does, transfer the bundle to a pan that can go on the grill (it's a good idea to have this handy, just in case) to finish the cooking. Depending on the heat of the grill and the size of the potatoes, cooking time is generally 30 to 40 minutes. You're looking for them to be tender and a wee bit crispy.

Mashed Potatoes

In my youth, mashed potatoes were on my family's dinner table more often than not. For me they are the ultimate in comfort food. I prefer yellow fleshed Yukon Gold potatoes for mashing, as they dry out well and stay light and fluffy.

2 lb Yukon Gold potatoes,
scrubbed and halved

1 Tbsp salt plus more to taste

1 cup whipping cream

2 Tbsp butter, cubed

Serves 4

In a heavy-bottomed pot, place the potatoes and cover with cold water. I keep the skins on, but peeled works too. Add 1 Tbsp of the salt and bring to a boil. Turn down the heat to a low boil and cook uncovered for 20 minutes, or until tender. Drain, and let them sit in the colander for a few minutes to ensure that all the excess water is drained off. Return the potatoes to the pot.

In a small saucepan, heat the cream for a few minutes until hot but not boiling.

Mash the potatoes using a potato masher, or, if you like them smooth and creamy, put them through a food mill or ricer. I like my mashed potatoes fluffy, with no lumps. Stay away from using an electric mixer or food processor as they result in a gluey consistency of mashed potatoes.

Fold in the hot cream and butter until well incorporated. Season with salt to taste.

Cornbread

Mom's kitchen was run on a tight budget when I was growing up, so this cornbread was the base of a lot of meals. We used to cover it with pinto beans, chopped onions and shredded cheese, but now I like it with a slab of butter next to a bowl of chowder. Leftover cornbread makes for wonderful turkey stuffing, or you can cube it and sauté it for croutons.

2 ¼ cups flour

1 cup sugar

¾ cup coarse cornmeal

2 tsp baking powder

2 tsp salt

5 eggs

1 ¼ cups buttermilk

¾ cup plus 1 Tbsp canola oil

½ tsp pure vanilla extract

1 cup frozen corn kernels, rinsed (see Cook's Note)

Serves 8

Preheat the oven to 400°F.

Heat an ovenproof cast iron frying pan, 6–8 inches in diameter, in the oven for 20 minutes.

While the frying pan is heating, mix the flour, sugar, cornmeal, baking powder and salt together in a large bowl.

In a separate bowl, whisk the eggs, buttermilk, ¾ cup canola oil and vanilla until frothy. Slowly fold the wet ingredients into the dry ingredients (there will be lumps), then stir in the corn.

Remove the hot frying pan from the oven and lightly oil with the 1 Tbsp of canola oil. Pour the batter into the frying pan to about three-quarters full and return to the oven for 25 minutes. Turn down the oven to 350°F and bake for an additional 15 minutes or until cooked all the way through. Test this by inserting a toothpick into the center of the bread—if it comes out clean you know it's ready.

Remove the cornbread from the oven and let it rest in the frying pan for 20 minutes before cutting.

. . . .

COOK'S NOTE: *Fresh corn does not work for this recipe. I've been making it for over 10 years now and at least once a year I give fresh corn another shot. But it always caramelizes, turns black and chewy and lets me down. Sometimes (only sometimes!) fresh isn't best after all.*

Honey Whole Wheat Buns or Loaves

This recipe is for a basic, soft wheat bun that goes well with many things (burgers, fish, cheese, BBQ or deli meats). If you'd prefer loaves, divide the dough in two and bake it in loaf pans—it makes killer breakfast toast.

3 cups warm water (warm to the touch but not hot, about 110°F)

⅔ cup plus 1 tsp honey

¼ cup plus 1 ½ tsp active dry yeast

4 cups flour

4 cups whole wheat flour

½ cup butter, melted

2 eggs

2 tsp salt

Canola oil or cooking spray, for greasing the pans

Makes 10 buns or 2 loaves

In a very large bowl, use a wooden spoon to mix together the water and 1 tsp of the honey with the yeast to form a sponge. The mixture will start to rise and thicken. Stop mixing and let it stand for 5 minutes.

Add 2 cups of the flour and 2 cups of the whole wheat flour and stir to combine. The dough will be loose like pancake batter. Let the dough stand and rise for 30 minutes.

Mix the remaining ⅔ cup honey, melted butter, eggs and salt into the dough. Slowly add and incorporate the remaining flour. Cover the bowl and let the dough rise in a warm, draft-free place for about 45 minutes.

Preheat the oven to 400°F.

To make buns, line a baking sheet with parchment paper. Shape the dough into 10 palm-sized balls. You want these to be uniform in shape, so roll them between your cupped palm and the countertop. If the dough is sticky, sprinkle a little flour on the countertop. Continue rolling until the dough ball is smooth and the bottom is sealed. Place the balls on the prepared baking sheet, 2 inches apart, and let them rest for 15 minutes. Bake in the center of the oven for 15 minutes until the buns make a hollow sound when you lightly tap the bottom.

To make loaves, lightly grease two 9- × 5-inch pans or two 8- × 4-inch pans with canola oil or cooking spray.

Divide the dough in two. Gently shape the dough so that it will fit inside the pans. You want to just lightly manipulate it here, just enough to pull it together and make sure there are no air bubbles inside. Let the dough rest on the countertop for 15 minutes. Transfer the dough to the pans and bake for 25 minutes.

. . . .

COOK'S NOTE: *I love seeds, so I often brush the bun dough with a light egg wash and scatter pumpkin seeds or sesame seeds on top just before they go into the oven.*

Desserts

Key Lime Pie 227

Blueberry Pie 228

Rhubarb Custard Pie 231

Strawberry and Rhubarb Crumble 234

Mascarpone Cheesecake with Roasted Strawberries and Fresh Mint Cream 237

Dark Chocolate and Salted Caramel Tart 239

Spiced Poached Pear and Quince Almond Tart 240

Salted Chocolate Bomb with Habanero Berry Compote 243

Oatmeal Chocolate Chip Cookies 245

Ginger Cookies 246

Flourless Chocolate Hazelnut Cookies 247

Key Lime Pie

This is the classic, staple dessert of Florida. There is only one way to make it and this is it.

1 ¼ cups graham cracker crumbs

¼ cup granulated sugar

½ cup butter, melted

6 egg yolks

Two 300 ml cans sweetened condensed milk (2 ½ cups)

¾ cup key lime juice (about 20 key limes)

3 cups whipping cream

2 Tbsp icing sugar

1 tsp pure vanilla extract

Serves 8–10

Preheat the oven to 350°F. Lightly butter a 9-inch pie dish.

In a medium-sized bowl, combine the graham cracker crumbs and sugar with the butter until it resembles wet sand. Press the mixture firmly and evenly into the bottom and sides of the prepared pie dish and bake in the center of the oven for 7 to 9 minutes. Remove and allow to cool for about 20 minutes. Leave the oven on.

In a separate bowl whisk the egg yolks lightly. Add the condensed milk and whisk to combine. Using a rubber spatula, stir in the key lime juice, ¼ cup at a time, stirring well after each addition. Pour the filling into the cooled pie crust. Bake for 5 to 7 minutes.

Let the pie cool completely, then refrigerate uncovered for at least 4 hours to set.

Place the whipping cream, icing sugar and vanilla in a medium-sized bowl and whip until soft peaks form.

To serve, slice the pie and top generously with whipped cream.

Blueberry Pie

BC is the number-one highbush blueberry-producing region in the world, and we like to celebrate that fact with pie!

1 double pie crust (see
Pie Pastry below)

8 cups fresh blueberries

¾ cup granulated sugar

Juice of 1 lemon

3 Tbsp cornstarch

½ tsp salt

Serves 8–10

. . . .

COOK'S NOTE: *This recipe can also be made with blackberries, though you'll need to cut the cornstarch down by half.*

Prepare the pie crusts and line a 9-inch pie pan with the bottom crust.

Preheat the oven to 400°F. Line a baking sheet with parchment paper.

In medium-sized bowl, place the blueberries, sugar, lemon juice, cornstarch and salt. Fill the bottom crust with this blueberry mixture. Lightly brush the edge of the crust with water.

Place the top pie crust over the filling and press all around the edges to seal. Using kitchen scissors, trim the excess crust to a 1 inch overhang, folding the dough under to form an edge. Using your fingers, crimp the dough along the rim of the pan. With a small knife, cut a few slits in the center of the pie to allow the steam to escape.

Place the pie on the prepared baking sheet, to catch any drips. Bake on the lowest rack of the oven for 20 minutes. Turn down the heat to 350°F, and move the pie to the middle rack. Bake for an additional 40 to 60 minutes, or until the crust is golden brown and the filling is thickened and bubbly. If the crust browns too quickly, loosely cover it with aluminum foil.

Let the pie cool for 1 to 2 hours on a rack before serving.

Pie Pastry

2 ½ cups flour

1 Tbsp granulated sugar

1 cup cold salted butter, cubed
(if using unsalted butter add
1 tsp salt to the flour mixture)

Makes 1 double pie crust (for a single pie crust, halve the recipe)

. . . .

COOK'S NOTE: *The pie pastry can be frozen for up to 1 month: wrap the dough balls or disks in plastic wrap and freeze until the day before baking, then thaw in the fridge overnight and roll as directed.*

In a large bowl stir together the flour and sugar. Add the butter and, using your hands, rub it into the flour mixture until the butter is in pea-sized bits, with some larger pieces. Add ¾ cup ice-cold water all at once and toss the mixture with your hands until a loose dough forms. Work the dough just enough so that it comes together, but do not overknead it.

With floured hands, press the pastry dough into two disks or balls. Wrap the pastry in plastic wrap and refrigerate for 1 hour or until well chilled.

Lightly flour a clean work surface and roll out one disk of dough into a 13-inch diameter circle. Transfer it to a 9-inch pie plate and trim the edges to be even with the plate. For double-crust recipes, roll out the second piece of pastry to a 13-inch diameter and follow the recipe method for how to seal the pie.

Rhubarb Custard Pie

Rhubarb is the first fresh spring pie ingredient we see here in BC. We get very excited knowing that just around the corner are strawberries and salmonberries. This recipe is based on an old Southern classic called chess pie. The custard is usually made from buttermilk, so the fat content is not quite as high as it is in other custard-type pies. My father loved chess pie and it always makes me a little weepy when I see one being made at SoBo. I wish that he could have seen what has happened to me and my love of sharing food. This one's for you, Dad.

1 single pie crust (see Pie Pastry page 228)

4–6 stalks rhubarb, diced small (about 2 cups)

3 egg yolks

1 ¼ cups granulated sugar

¼ cup cornmeal or flour

¼ tsp salt

1 cup buttermilk

¼ cup unsalted butter, melted

2 Tbsp lemon juice (1 medium lemon)

Serves 8

Prepare the pie pastry and line a 9-inch pie pan with it. Preheat the oven to 400°F.

Spread the diced rhubarb over the bottom of the pie shell.

In a medium-sized bowl, whisk the egg yolks until frothy, 1 to 2 minutes. Add the sugar, cornstarch and salt then the buttermilk, melted butter and lemon juice and whisk until well combined.

Pour the egg mixture into the pie shell and bake for 10 minutes. Turn down the oven to 325°F and bake for 40 minutes more. If the pie crust is browning too quickly, tent some foil over the top for the last 20 minutes or so.

Remove from the oven and let the pie cool before serving. A dusting of powdered icing sugar on top will add a bit of sweetness if you find the pie a little tart.

232

Winter

Tofino is famous for its storm season. Waves—en route from Asia with nothing in the way to stop them—come crashing onto the coastline with a 20-foot purpose. Only a handful of Tofino's best surfers dare to paddle out into the big stuff, and the international riders are smart enough to just sit, watch and be amazed (it's too cold for most people, anyway!). The busiest square footage in most kitchens is the freezer area, where the bounty of spring, summer and fall is stored, ready to be called into action at an order's notice. Crab fishermen are still active, but largely fishing goes to ground. Only the oysters, clams and mussels are being harvested as they are now at their absolute peak. As winter takes hold, nearly the whole town turns out for the annual Clayoquot Oyster Festival, a richly decorated barnburner with shucking competitions, mermaid costumes and dancing well past everyone's bedtime. Not to mention the consumption of over 10,000 oysters (and not a few bottles of wine) supplied by more than a dozen chef stations serving oysters in myriad delicious ways.

Strawberry and Rhubarb Crumble

I just love rhubarb! I remember being a young girl—probably around five years old—and it was growing in the backyard. I would lie next to a weeping willow and just chew on the stalks, loving the tartness.

1 single pie crust (see
Pie Pastry page 228)

1 ½ cups packed brown sugar

½ cup plus 3 Tbsp flour

½ tsp salt

¼ cup plus 2 tsp cold unsalted butter

3 eggs

3 Tbsp whipping cream

4 cups trimmed and roughly chopped
rhubarb stalks (10–12 stalks) (frozen
and thawed can also be used)

1 cup quartered strawberries

½ cup rolled oats

1 tsp ground cinnamon

½ tsp grated nutmeg

Serves 8–10

Prepare the pie crust and line a 9-inch pie pan with it. Preheat the oven to 375°F. Line a baking sheet with parchment paper.

In a large bowl, mix together 1 cup of the brown sugar, 3 Tbsp of the flour and the salt with the 2 tsp butter.

In a small bowl, whisk together the eggs and cream.

Add the rhubarb, berries and egg mixture to the dry mixture. Using a wooden spoon, combine well. Scoop into the pie shell and even out.

Prepare the crumble topping by blending the remaining ½ cup brown sugar, ½ cup flour and ¼ cup butter with the oats, cinnamon and nutmeg using a wooden spoon. You should get a nice crumbly texture (hence the name of this pie). Sprinkle the crumble mixture on top of the filling.

Place the pie pan on the prepared baking sheet to catch any drips and bake for 45 to 60 minutes, until bubbly and crisp.

Allow to cool for at least 1 hour before serving. I love my crumble served with a single scoop of vanilla ice cream.

Mascarpone Cheesecake
with Roasted Strawberries and Fresh Mint Cream

Second only to a bowl of chocolate ice cream, cheesecake has remained my dessert of choice since I was a wee girl. I can still remember the sweet satisfaction I felt when I tasted my first true New York–style cheesecake (and not the boxed version that dominated grocery store shelves in the 1960s and 1970s): It was at one of my first waitress jobs, in Fort Worth, and once a week I would treat myself to a slice. We only recently added this to the menu at SoBo, and I love that we can serve it year-round because of how gloriously the frozen strawberries roast up. This cheesecake is best made the day before serving.

Cheesecake

1 cup graham cracker crumbs

2 Tbsp brown sugar

⅓ cup butter, melted

2 cups cream cheese, room temperature

1 ¼ cups granulated sugar

1 tsp pure vanilla extract

5 eggs

2 cups mascarpone cheese, room temperature

Topping

4 cups strawberries, hulled and left whole

½ cup plus 2 Tbsp granulated sugar

1 vanilla bean

1 ½ cups whipping cream

½ cup fresh mint leaves

Serves 12

Cheesecake

Preheat the oven to 350°F. Grease the bottom of a 9-inch springform pan with a little butter or cooking spray.

In a medium-sized bowl and using a wooden spoon, stir the graham cracker crumbs and sugar with the melted butter to combine. Press the mixture firmly and evenly into the bottom of the prepared pan. Bake for 5 minutes. Remove from the oven and let it cool. Keep the oven on.

In a food processor, mix the cream cheese with the granulated sugar—add the sugar slowly as the mixer runs, stopping occasionally to scrape down the sides of the bowl. Mix until smooth and be sure there are no lumps in the batter. Add the vanilla, then the eggs one at a time, mixing well after each addition. Add the mascarpone cheese and mix again.

Pour the batter into the cooled pie shell. Return to the oven and bake for 20 minutes. Turn down the oven to 300°F and bake for 20 to 30 minutes, until the cheesecake is still slightly jiggly in the very middle.

Remove the cheesecake from the oven and run a sharp knife around the outside edge to loosen it from the pan. Let it sit at room temperature undisturbed until it has cooled, about 2 hours, then cover and chill overnight in the fridge.

Topping

Place the strawberries in a medium bowl with the ½ cup of sugar. Split the vanilla bean lengthwise and use the point of a paring knife to scrape the seeds into the bowl. Add the bean. Stir to coat the berries in sugar and seeds. Let them sit for 1 hour at room temperature to liquefy the sugar and meld the flavors.

Preheat the oven to 300°F. Line a baking sheet with parchment paper.

continued on next page

Transfer the mixture to the prepared baking sheet. Roast the berries for 1 hour, stirring them every 15 minutes. The strawberries should be soft, fragrant and syrupy when they are done. Remove from the oven and set aside.

Meanwhile, in a small saucepan over low heat, bring ½ cup of the whipping cream to a simmer. Remove from the heat and add the mint leaves. Let the cream steep for 20 minutes at room temperature, then strain through a fine mesh sieve and chill until cold.

Add the chilled mint cream to a mixing bowl with the remaining 1 cup whipping cream. Whip until soft peaks form. Add the remaining 2 Tbsp sugar and whip until the cream is medium-soft. Keep this chilled until you are ready to use.

Top the cheesecake with roasted strawberries and a dollop of minted cream and serve.

Dark Chocolate and Salted Caramel Tart

I have had the good fortune to work with Jen Scott, our pastry chef, for nearly a decade—in which time she has come to know Artie's insatiable sweet tooth! This delightful, sinfully rich tart was created in his honor. It's starting to develop a cult-like following.

Tart Shell (page 241)

1 ½ cups whipping cream

1 cup granulated sugar

5 Tbsp water

2 pinches sea salt, plus
extra for serving

1 cup bittersweet chocolate chips
or dark chocolate pieces

**Serves 10–12 (cut thin slices, as the
tart is very rich)**

Prepare the tart shell and set aside to cool.

In a small saucepan over medium-high heat, bring ½ cup of the whipping cream to a boil. Turn off the heat.

In a separate saucepan over high heat, combine the sugar with the water and cook, stirring, until the sugar dissolves, 3 to 4 minutes. Bring the mixture to a boil and let it cook, without stirring, for about 4 minutes, until it achieves a dark amber color. It's important not to stir the mixture as it makes the sugar stick together. You can swirl the pan to help get any uncooked sugar melting if necessary. Take the pan off the heat.

Slowly and very carefully whisk the warm cream into the caramel. Stand back as you pour in the cream as it will spit back. Stir until smooth, then add a pinch of salt. If the mixture is not smooth, return it to the pan over low heat and stir gently with a wooden spoon.

Carefully pour the caramel into the prepared tart shell, evenly covering the bottom. Let it cool for about 10 minutes.

In a medium-sized mixing bowl, place the chocolate and 2 pinches of the salt.

In a small saucepan over medium heat, bring the remaining 1 cup cream to a boil. Pour the cream over the chocolate, let it sit for 3 minutes and then whisk gently until smooth. Spoon the chocolate over the caramel layer in the tart shell to about ¼ inch thick. Allow the chocolate to set at room temperature for at least 3 hours.

Sprinkle the tart with a little more sea salt and serve.

Spiced Poached Pear
and Quince Almond Tart

In fall, when quince and pears start ripening on the trees, I get a warm tingle in my blood. I can't put my finger on exactly why; all I know is that quince really excites me. Maybe it's the combination of the hard fuzzy exterior and the shockingly beautiful pinkish flesh that is produced after cooking?

Tart

Tart Shell (page 241)

2 cups granulated sugar

3 Tbsp lemon juice (1 medium lemon)

2 star anise

1 cinnamon stick, broken into pieces

3 pears, peeled and cored

1 quince, peeled and cored

Frangipane

6 Tbsp unsalted butter,
room temperature

¼ cup icing sugar

¾ cup ground almonds

2 Tbsp flour

1 egg, beaten

Serves 8

Prepare the tart shell and set aside to cool.

In a large saucepan over low heat, bring 4 cups water plus the sugar, lemon juice, star anise and cinnamon stick to a simmer and let simmer for 5 minutes.

Meanwhile, prepare the fruit. Cut the pears in half and the quince into quarters. In the saucepan containing the sugar and spices, poach the pears at a light simmer for 5 to 10 minutes, depending on their ripeness (the less ripe they are, the longer they need). Next poach the quince pieces, in the same pot, until tender, about 15 to 25 minutes. Reserve the poaching liquid when you remove the fruit from the pan. Let the fruit cool, then cut it into ¼-inch slices.

Place 1 cup of the poaching liquid in a small saucepan. Bring it to a boil and simmer, uncovered, until the mixture is reduced by half. Remove from the heat and set aside.

For the frangipane (the almond cream filling), in a large mixing bowl, cream the butter and icing sugar together with a mixer or whisk until smooth. Stir in the ground almonds and flour. Slowly add the beaten egg to the almond mixture. Stir until well incorporated.

Preheat the oven to 350°F.

Spread 1½ Tbsp of the frangipane over the bottom of the tart shell. Arrange the fruit slices evenly over the frangipane base and spread the remaining frangipane over top.

Bake the tart for 10 to 15 minutes to set the filling. Remove from the oven and let cool. To finish, drizzle a spoonful or so of the reduced poaching liquid over the fruit.

Tart Shell

½ cup butter, slightly softened

¾ cup icing sugar

2 egg yolks, cold

1 ¾ cups flour

¼ tsp salt

2 Tbsp ice-cold water

Makes one 10-inch tart shell

In a stand mixer fitted with the paddle attachment, cream the butter with the icing sugar. Add the egg yolks and mix well. Reduce the mixer speed to low, and add the flour, salt and water. Continue to mix until the dough just comes together. Wrap the dough in plastic wrap and chill in the refrigerator for 1 hour.

When the dough is chilled, lightly flour the work surface and use a rolling pin to roll it out into a big circle, about 12 inches wide and ⅛ inch thick. Chill for another 20 minutes in the refrigerator. If the dough gets too warm during the rolling process, it will be impossible to achieve a light, flaky pastry.

Preheat the oven to 375°F.

Transfer the dough to a 10-inch tart pan and then cover it with a layer of parchment paper. Fill the tart pan with a layer of pie weights (ceramic beans or dried beans) to weigh down the dough and prevent it from rising unevenly. Bake for 8 to 10 minutes. Remove from the oven, and remove the pie weights and parchment paper. Return to the oven and bake for another 3 to 5 minutes, until golden. Remove from the oven and allow to cool in the pan.

Salted Chocolate Bomb
with Habanero Berry Compote

Sometimes I miss living on the border with Mexico and always seeing, tasting and smelling that fantastic combination of salt, chocolate and spice. A lot of customers were caught off guard when we first put this on the menu—because the salt/spice/chocolate combo was so rare back then—and some even thought the kitchen had made a mistake! I can't imagine a more suitable Valentine's Day dessert, so if your sweetheart is deserving, take a day and blow their mind with this treat.

Cake

1 cup bittersweet chocolate chips or dark chocolate pieces

1 Tbsp butter

4 eggs plus 2 egg yolks

⅓ cup granulated sugar

¾ cup whipping cream

1 Tbsp fleur de sel (for garnish)

Mousse

1 ½ cups bittersweet chocolate chips or dark chocolate pieces

2 eggs

2 ¾ cups whipping cream

Ganache

1 ¾ cups bittersweet chocolate chips or dark chocolate pieces

1 ½ cups whipping cream

Berry Compote

4 cups fresh or frozen berries (ideally blueberries, blackberries or raspberries, but most any berries will do)

⅓ cup granulated sugar

⅛ tsp habanero chili powder

Serves 10–12

Cake

Preheat the oven to 400°F. Butter a 9-inch springform cake pan and line the bottom with parchment paper.

Either use a double boiler or fill a small saucepan halfway with water and bring it to a boil on the stovetop. Place a stainless steel bowl on top of the saucepan, leaving enough room so that the water doesn't touch the bottom of the bowl. Add the chocolate and the butter to the bowl and melt it over the boiling water. Set aside the chocolate but keep the saucepan filled with water. Replenish with more water if needed and return to a boil.

In a larger stainless steel bowl, combine the eggs, yolks and sugar. Set the bowl on top of the saucepan of water. With a wire whisk, whip the egg mixture over the hot water until it is thickened and warm, about 10 minutes. It should triple in volume. Remove from the heat.

Stir the melted chocolate into the egg mixture in two batches, as it will be very thick. Continue to stir the mixture until it is cool to the touch but not cold, about 5 minutes.

In a separate bowl, using a mixer or a whisk, whip the cream until soft peaks are formed. Gently fold half the whipped cream into the chocolate mixture and then fold in the second half. Pour this into the prepared cake pan.

Place the cake pan inside a larger pan, and add hot water to the large pan until it reaches halfway up the exterior of the cake pan walls. Bake for 25 minutes or until the cake is crusty on top and firm to the touch.

Remove from the oven and allow to cool for 30 minutes before inverting it onto a baking sheet. Refrigerate until cold, about 1 hour.

continued on next page

COOK'S NOTE: *The temperature of the ganache is very important. A thermometer is best for accuracy, but I was taught to test for temperature against my top lip—you want the ganache to be just cool to the touch, a little cooler than room temperature. If it becomes too cold, you will have to heat it back up again and repeat the cooling process until you get it right.*

Mousse

Melt the chocolate the same way as you did for the cake. Set aside.

Set another bowl on top of the saucepan of water. Using a wire whisk, whip the eggs over the hot water until they are warm. Fold half of the chocolate into the eggs, mix gently, and then add the other half.

In a separate bowl, whip the cream to medium peaks. Fold half the whipped cream into the chocolate mixture. Fold in the other half.

Place the cooled cake back into the cake pan. Pour the chocolate mousse over the top of it, smoothing the surface with a spatula. Lightly tap the pan on the counter to settle the mousse.

Freeze for several hours or overnight. This will help with icing the bomb.

Ganache

Place the chocolate in a medium-sized bowl.

In a medium-sized saucepan over medium heat, heat the whipping cream until it just comes to a boil. Pour the hot cream over the chocolate. Let it sit for a few minutes, then stir gently until well combined. Cool the ganache to 90°F, about 5 minutes.

Remove the cake from the fridge and then from the cake pan, and place it on a rack over a baking sheet.

Starting at the center, pour the ganache over the cake, letting it drip down to cover the sides. Any ganache left on the baking sheet can be reused, until the cake is evenly covered. Chill until serving time.

Berry Compote

Place half the berries with the sugar and chili powder in a small saucepan. If you are using fresh berries, add a little water to prevent them from scorching.

Heat the berries over medium heat until the mixture begins to boil. Lower the heat to a simmer and cook the berries until soft. Remove the saucepan from the heat and let cool slightly, 5 minutes.

Place the warm berries in a medium-mesh sieve set over a clean mixing bowl. Use a wooden spoon to force them through the sieve to remove the seeds and pulp.

Place the remaining 2 cups of berries in a small bowl and pour the warm, strained berries over them. Stir, cover and set aside until ready to serve.

To Serve

Use a hot dry knife to cut the cake into 10–12 pieces. Pool some compote in the center of each plate and place a slice of cake on top. Sprinkle fleur de sel sparingly on top of the bomb.

Oatmeal Chocolate Chip Cookies

These old-fashioned cookies are the perfect balance of crispy and chewy and are the top-selling cookie at SoBo. Admittedly, with so many people discovering they have a gluten allergy, the Flourless Chocolate Hazelnut Cookies (page 247) are gaining on them fast. But can you really go wrong when it comes to cookie choices? Nope.

¾ cup chopped walnuts

1 cup salted butter, room temperature

1 cup packed brown sugar

1 cup granulated sugar

2 eggs

2 Tbsp water

1 tsp pure vanilla extract

1 ½ cups flour

1 tsp baking soda

1 tsp salt

1 tsp ground cinnamon

3 cups rolled oats

1 ¼ cups semi-sweet chocolate chips

Makes 20 large cookies
See photo on page 224

Preheat the oven to 375°F.

Arrange the chopped walnuts on a baking sheet and toast them in the oven for 5 minutes. Set aside to cool. Turn off the oven.

Use a mixer or whisk to cream the butter and both the sugars together in a large bowl until light and fluffy. Slowly beat in the eggs, water and vanilla until they are incorporated.

In a separate bowl, whisk together the flour, baking soda, salt and cinnamon, then slowly add to the creamed butter using the low setting on the mixer. Using a wooden spoon, stir in the nuts, oats and chocolate chips until a stiff dough is formed.

Cover the bowl with plastic wrap and let the dough sit at room temperature for 1 hour.

Preheat the oven to 350°F. Line a baking sheet with parchment paper.

Using an ice cream scoop, scoop balls of dough onto the prepared baking sheet, 2 inches apart. Gently press down on the dough a little with your hand. This is your chance to decide if you want to make them thin and crispy or thick and chewy.

Bake in the center of the oven for 9 to 11 minutes, until golden around the edges. Remove the cookies and let them cool for 5 minutes on the baking sheet before transferring them to racks to cool completely. Store in an airtight container for up to 3 days, or freeze for up to 3 months.

Ginger Cookies

Ginger cookies always remind me of the holidays, but these babies are on the menu all year! The caramelized ginger adds a perfect bite to the rich spice, and the little dip in sugar gives a crunch to these otherwise soft and chewy treats.

1 cup unsalted butter,
room temperature

½ cup granulated sugar

½ cup packed brown sugar

1 egg

⅓ cup molasses

2 ¼ cups flour

2 tsp baking powder

2 tsp ground ginger

1 tsp ground cinnamon

½ tsp ground allspice

¼ cup chopped crystallized
ginger (optional)

½ cup raw sugar

Makes 24 (or 12 SoBo-sized) cookies
See photo on page 224

Use a mixer or whisk to cream the butter with the granulated and brown sugars in a large bowl until light and fluffy. Beat in the egg and molasses until incorporated.

In a separate bowl, stir together the flour, baking soda, ground ginger, cinnamon and allspice then slowly add them to the creamed butter, with the mixer running on low. Remove the bowl from the mixer and fold in the crystallized ginger if using.

Cover the bowl with plastic wrap and refrigerate the dough for 1 hour.

Preheat the oven to 350°F. Line a baking sheet with parchment paper.

Place the raw sugar in a small bowl. Using an ice cream scoop, scoop up balls of cold dough and roll them in the raw sugar. Set them 2 inches apart on the prepared baking sheet and flatten them slightly with your hand. Bake in the center of the oven for 10 to 12 minutes, until firm.

Remove the cookies from the oven and let cool for 5 minutes on the baking sheet before transferring them to racks to cool completely. Store in an airtight container for up to 3 days, or freeze for up to 3 months.

. . . .

COOK'S NOTE: *Raw sugar is natural sugar cane pressed into crystals. The molasses is left in, giving it an amber shade. I like the texture it provides for baking, and it contains some trace nutrient and minerals.*

Flourless Chocolate Hazelnut Cookies

Our gluten-free customers swear by these! If you like ice cream sandwiches as much as our kids do, slather a big scoop of high-quality ice cream between two of these monsters!

1 ½ cups whole hazelnuts

3 cups icing sugar

¾ cup Dutch-style cocoa powder

½ tsp salt

¾ cup dark chocolate chunks or chips

4 egg whites

2 tsp pure vanilla extract

Makes 10–12 large cookies

See photo on page 224

Preheat the oven to 350°F. Line a baking sheet with parchment paper.

Arrange the hazelnuts on the prepared baking sheet and bake for 5 minutes. Remove from the oven, let cool for about 3 minutes then place them on a clean kitchen towel and give them a good rub to remove the skins. Set aside.

In a large bowl, sift together the icing sugar, cocoa powder and salt. Add the chocolate chunks and hazelnuts and stir to incorporate.

In a small bowl, lightly mix together the egg whites and vanilla with a fork. Stir the egg mixture into the cocoa mixture. It may look like you will need more egg whites but just keep stirring until no dry ingredients show on the chocolate pieces or the nuts and the batter comes together. The batter will be loose and look wet.

Using an ice cream scoop, scoop balls of dough onto the prepared baking sheet, 2 inches apart.

Bake in the center of the oven for 10 minutes, or until the surface of the cookies appear dry and cracked. Remove from the oven and allow to cool completely on the baking sheet before serving. Store in an airtight container for up to 3 days, or freeze for up to 3 months.

Staple Recipes

Stocks

How long do I have for this subject? I could go on about stocks for ages. I feel very strongly about the hows and whys of stocks; they are a great way of honoring a no-waste, nose-to-tail philosophy.

By just following a few simple rules, you can have clear, rich, flavorful stock each and every time for a fraction of what you would spend on the packaged kind. Make sure to use good vegetables (not roots and peels) and cold, fresh water (never hot water that has gone through the hot water element thing); and make sure to always turn the stock down to a simmer as soon as it reaches boiling point. The lazy bubble is a stock's best friend. Skimming is also crucial, as is never, ever using burned bones. I am often surprised to find cooks over-roasting bones or mirepoix, thinking that it won't affect the outcome. But it will, and not positively!

Vegetable Stock

This is a truly invaluable ingredient in my kitchen. I only use vegetable stocks in my vegetable soups. The idea of using chicken stock in say, an asparagus soup, has never really sat well with me. It's easier, for sure, to impart flavor with a rich chicken broth, but when dining out or at a friend's home for dinner, vegetarians are often unknowingly consuming animal products they would otherwise rather avoid. I'm not keen on tricking either my friends or customers, and what's wrong with asparagus soup tasting like asparagus?

¼ cup olive oil

8 yellow onions, chopped

3 large carrots, chopped

2–3 large leeks, greens only, chopped

8 stalks celery, chopped

2 cups chopped vegetables (optional, see Cook's Note)

1 cup dry white wine

6 quarts cold water

2 Tbsp salt

2 bay leaves

3–5 sprigs of fresh herbs such as flat-leaf parsley, marjoram, oregano or thyme

Makes 4 quarts

Heat the oil in a large, heavy-bottomed stockpot on low to medium heat. Sauté the onions, carrots, leeks and celery for about 20 minutes, or until tender. Add the optional vegetables if using.

Add the wine and let it evaporate, 3 to 4 minutes. Add the water, and then the salt, bay leaves and fresh herbs. Bring to a boil, turn down to a lazy bubble and simmer uncovered for 45 minutes. Skim off any foam that rises to the top.

Strain the stock immediately and cool it down as quickly as possible (see sidebar). This stock stays fresh for 4 to 5 days. If you can't use it within a few days, you can freeze it in small containers and thaw it out as needed.

. . . .

COOK'S NOTE: *If I were using this stock in asparagus soup I would use the woody stalks of asparagus in the stock. If I wanted a corn-flavored stock I would use the corn cobs, mushroom stems for mushroom stock, etc. Avoid strongly flavored vegetables like cabbage, broccoli and beets.*

Chicken Stock

2 Tbsp canola oil

2 onions, chopped

2 stalks celery, chopped

2 carrots, chopped

6 quarts cold water

2 ½ lb assorted chicken necks, backs and wings (fresh or roasted)

10 sprigs fresh flat-leaf parsley

2 bay leaves

1 tsp salt

¼ tsp whole black peppercorns

Makes 4 quarts

Heat the oil in a large, heavy bottomed stockpot over medium heat. Add the onions, celery and carrots. Sweat for 20 minutes until all the vegetables are soft.

Add the cold water, chicken, parsley, bay leaves, salt and peppercorns. Bring to a boil, turn down to a lazy bubble and let simmer uncovered for about 3 hours, skimming the fat off regularly.

Strain through a fine mesh sieve and let cool (see sidebar). This stock keeps for 6 to 7 days in the fridge. Freeze what you can't use within a few days.

COOK'S NOTE: *For a darker, richer chicken stock, add 1 cup tomato paste and 1 cup dry white wine after sweating the vegetables. Stir and cook for another 10 minutes before adding the water and herbs.*

Fish Stock

½ cup olive oil

2 carrots, chopped

2 stalks celery, chopped

1 yellow onion, chopped

1 large leek, greens only, chopped

4 lb fish bones and trimmings

2 cups dry white wine

6 quarts cold water

2 Tbsp salt

6 peppercorns, cracked

4 sprigs fresh thyme

2 bay leaves

Makes 4 quarts

Heat the oil in a large stockpot over medium heat. Add the carrots, celery, onion and leek and sauté for 10 minutes. Add the fish and sauté for another 5 minutes. Add the wine and cook, stirring occasionally, for an additional 5 minutes.

Add the water, salt, peppercorns, thyme and bay leaves. Bring to a boil, turn down to a lazy bubble and simmer uncovered for 1 ½ hours.

Strain and use right away or chill down (see sidebar). This stock will last for 5 days in the fridge, and freezes beautifully.

Chilling Stock and Soups

To chill stocks and soups down quickly, strain them into a container of your choice, then submerge the container into a sink filled with ice water for 1 hour or so. Stir the stock/soup every once in a while. You never want to put piping hot stock/soup into the fridge as it will change the temperature in the fridge and possibly spoil other foods around it.

Roasted Garlic

There are different ways to roast garlic. The first is to use whole heads; the second is to use peeled cloves.

ROASTING WHOLE HEADS: Preheat the oven to 400°F. Cut the papery (non-root) end off the garlic head, exposing just a peek of the cloves. Lightly drizzle the garlic with 2 Tbsp olive oil and wrap tightly in aluminum foil. Place the wrapped garlic on a baking sheet and roast in the oven for 20 to 25 minutes, until soft enough to just push the cloves out of the skins, like toothpaste.

ROASTING PEELED CLOVES: Place the peeled cloves in a sauccpan, cover them with olive oil (about ½ tsp per clove) and simmer on medium-low heat for 15 minutes, or until tender. Strain off the oil and keep it for cooking other recipes (it will be garlic-flavored and can be kept refrigerated for up to 2 weeks).

Purée or chop the softened garlic for use. Always refrigerate roasted garlic. It will last for up to 1 week.

Roasted Chilies and Peppers

Roasting chilies and peppers is easy and adds a lot of depth to dishes. The idea is to char the skins until blackened but to not burn the chilies or peppers too deeply. There are several different methods: roast them on a BBQ grill, or with a gas stove flame or on a baking sheet in a very hot oven.

BBQ: Preheat the grill to high. Lay the chilies or peppers directly on to the racks, turning often for even roasting.

GAS STOVE: Turn on the flame and hold the chilies or peppers over the flame using metal tongs, turning them often, like you would a hot dog over a fire pit.

OVEN: Preheat the oven to 500°F. Place the chilies or peppers on a baking sheet and roast for 10 to 15 minutes.

When the chilies or peppers are blackened, place them in a bowl and cover tightly with plastic wrap. Let them sit for 20 minutes. This will steam them, making the skins easier to peel off. The skins should come off easily just by running your fingers along them.

Fire-Roasted Corn

Who doesn't love corn on the cob? It's just fun food—sweet, crunchy, juicy, summer glory! The corn season is short so I don't waste any time before I start freezing my fair share away for winter. Ideally corn is harvested in the morning and eaten before sundown. I know that's not always an option, but it's something to keep in mind when buying: the quality of the corn suffers with each passing day, so eat or freeze it right after purchasing.

1 ear of corn = ½ cup kernels

ROASTING BY BBQ: Soak the fresh corn on the cob in its husk for 1 hour in cold water. When you are ready to cook it, heat the BBQ to medium-high. Leave the corn in its husk and place it directly onto the grill. Cook for about 10 minutes, turning frequently to avoid burning. Pull back the husks and enjoy!

ROASTING IN THE OVEN: Preheat the oven to 450°F. Soak the corn on the cob in its husk for 1 hour in cold water. Leave the corn in its husk and place it on a baking sheet. Roast in the oven for 20 minutes.

REMOVING THE KERNELS: This can be a bit tricky, so be careful. The most important step is to balance the cob so it doesn't move. To do this, hold the corn upright on a cutting board in one hand, and run your knife in a sweeping downward motion to remove the kernels from the cob. Don't cut too close to the cob or you'll get the tough bits that stick in your teeth.

· ·

COOK'S NOTE: *Roasting and freezing corn can be fun as a group effort with one person shucking the roasted corn, one person cutting it from the cob and one person filling up freezer bags. Corn can be kept in the freezer for 6 months. I save my discarded cobs for vegetable stock.*

Dill Pickles

Say yes to homemade pickles and you can make them exactly as you like by playing around with the amount of garlic, chili and spice in the recipe. Once you're used to pickling, share your creations with friends, or throw a pickling party where everyone works in an assembly line and shares the end result. Throughout my life, I have got great pleasure from preserving food with family and friends.

2 cups white wine vinegar

2 cups water

2 cups pickling salt

12 small, pickling cucumbers (leave these whole or cut them to fit the mouth of the jar)

4–6 dried red Thai chilies or 1 tsp chili flakes

3 cloves garlic

4 tsp dill seed or 1 cup fresh dill, long stalks with flowering tops

Makes 4 (2 cup/500 ml) jars

Sterilize the jars and lids and keep them warm (see page 257).

In a medium-sized saucepan, bring the vinegar, water and salt to a boil to create a brine.

Divide the cucumbers, chilies, garlic and dill evenly between the jars, leaving about ½ inch at the top of each for the brine. Pour the hot brine into the jars until everything is covered. Screw on the lids.

Place a rack or tea towel in the bottom of a large pot (this prevents the jars from touching the bottom of the hot pot and breaking). Using canning tongs, place the jars in the pot, and fill it with enough hot water to cover the jars. Slowly bring to a boil and boil for 10 to 15 minutes. Using the canning tongs again, transfer the jars to a cooling rack and let them sit undisturbed for 24 hours. The pickles should be stored in a cool, dark, dry place, and should last for 6 to 12 months. Once open, store in the fridge for up to 1 month.

. . . .

COOK'S NOTE: *Don't be alarmed if the garlic turns green. It happens sometimes. It's important to use pickling salt rather than table salt, as iodized salts have anti-caking agents which turn the pickles cloudy. If you want to skip boiling the filled jars, allow the brine to cool completely before putting the lid on and then refrigerate. Store the pickles in the fridge for up to 6 months if you choose this option.*

Pickled Jalapeños

Pickled jalapeños are as common a condiment in Texas as ketchup is in Canada. You can add them to tacos, burgers, nachos, eggs and pizza (a plain cheese pizza with pickled jalapeños is the bomb!). A veggie taco (page 108) is just not complete without them. Everyone has their own family recipe in Texas; ours is a sweet version much like a bread and butter pickle. We use them so much we keep them in the fridge instead of canning them. They last for up to a year in the fridge. Art and Lina Nugteren from A&L Gardens grow jalapeños and we pickle for the entire month of October when their jalapeños are at their peak.

2 cups apple cider vinegar

½ cup sugar

16 jalapeño peppers with seeds, sliced crosswise

1 large yellow onion, sliced

2 medium carrots, julienned

1 medium red bell pepper, julienned

¼ cup pickling spice (I like a blend of bay leaves, coriander, mustard seeds and black peppercorns)

Makes 3 (1 cup/250 ml) jars (but you can use any container you want to store them in)

Pour the vinegar and sugar into a large heavy-bottomed pot, bring to a boil and reduce uncovered for 30 minutes.

Add the jalapeños to the boiling liquid and turn down the heat to medium. After 10 minutes, add the onion and continue to cook for 10 minutes. Add the carrot and bell pepper and cook for an additional 10 minutes.

Remove from the heat and add the pickling spice. Allow to cool in an out-of-the-way area as the pickling spice can irritate your lungs and eyes. I usually put them in the garage for an hour or so. Once cooled, put the jalapeños with all of their liquid into sterilized jars (see sidebar page 257) or containers of your choice and store in the fridge.

. . . .

COOK'S NOTE: *Once, a while back, I brought a jar of these peppers to a Christmas gift exchange and they were the most sought-after item that night. It was so much fun to see how many folks wanted those simple little peppers! If the sweet style of this recipe is not for you, you can omit the sugar and add 1 cup water and ¼ cup salt. If you like a hotter chili, serranos make a nice substitute.*

Fruit Chutney

Chutneys really jazz food up. We like to bake brie in filo and serve it with chutney and crostini. Roasted chicken goes well with a little chutney on the side, too. It's hard to predict exactly how much chutney this recipe will produce as the natural moisture in the apples varies every time. I like using Granny Smith, Ambrosia or Macintosh apples for this chutney, rather than Rome Beauty or Red Delicious. For pears I'd recommend Bartlett or Seckel. If you'd rather make the chutney with just one type of fruit, simply double the quantity asked of the fruit you like, and leave the other one out.

4 apples, peeled and cut into ½-inch chunks

6 pears, unpeeled and cut into ½-inch chunks

4 cups apple cider vinegar

4 cups packed dark brown sugar

4 large white onions, diced

2 medium red bell peppers, diced

2 cups raisins

1 Tbsp yellow mustard seeds

1 Tbsp salt

1 tsp ground cinnamon

1 tsp ground coriander

1 tsp ground cumin

1 tsp Madras curry powder

Makes 10–12 (1 cup/250 ml) jars

Place all the ingredients in a large saucepan and bring to a boil, stirring occasionally. Turn the heat down and simmer uncovered until thick, about 1 hour. Stir frequently as the chutney thickens to prevent it from scorching.

Fill hot 1-cup canning jars (see sidebar) with the chutney, leaving ½ inch of space at the top of each jar. Cover with hot, sterilized lids and screw the lid bands on tight.

Place a rack or tea towel in the bottom of a large pot (this prevents the jars from touching the bottom of the hot pot and breaking). Using canning tongs, place the jars in the pot, and fill it with enough hot water to cover the jars. Slowly bring to a boil and boil for 10 minutes. Using the canning tongs again, transfer the jars to a cooling rack and let them sit undisturbed for 24 hours. The chutney should be stored unopened in a cool dry place, and will last for 6 to 12 months. Once open, store in the fridge for up to 1 month.

Sterilizing Jars

The rule of thumb when deciding if jars should be sterilized depends on whether the recipe calls for the jars to be boiled in hot water after they have been filled. If they have to be boiled once filled, then there is no need to sterilize them first as they should become sterile during the boiling process. However, I would recommend always sterilizing the lids. Sterilizing both jars and lids is straightforward: Bring a large pot of water to a boil and carefully submerge the lids and jars in the water. Pull them out after 3 minutes or so, using clean tongs, and place them on a rack to air-dry. If I need to heat my lids or jars up, I generally run them through the dishwasher on the dry cycle, which gets them nice and hot.

Peach Preserves

Outside Fort Worth, Texas, is a little county called Parker County. And let me tell you, there is no touching a Parker County peach—sorry, Georgia and the Okanagan, that's just the way it is! Still, a juicy peach from somewhere else is better than no peach at all, so make this preserve with the best peaches you can find. Capture their summertime goodness and there will be smiles all around when you open a jar later in the year.

8 cups ½-inch chunks fresh peeled peaches (about 3 lb)

4 cups granulated sugar

3 Tbsp lemon juice (1 medium lemon)

Makes 6 (1 cup/250 ml) jars

Place all the ingredients in a large pot over medium-high heat. Bring to a boil and simmer uncovered for 30 minutes. At this point you should begin to check the preserves for consistency. To do this, chill a few small plates in the freezer. Drop 1 tsp of the hot preserves on a chilled plate. Return the plate to the freezer for a minute, and then tilt the plate to see if the liquid runs or not. The preserves should be soft with little liquid. If the mixture is still runny, continue to simmer. Repeat the consistency test every 5 to 10 minutes until a soft set is reached, 45 to 60 minutes in total.

Once the preserves are ready, it's time to start the canning process. Fill hot 1-cup (250 ml) canning jars with the preserve, leaving ¼ inch of space near the top of the jar. Cover with hot, sterilized lids and screw the lid bands on tight (see sidebar page 257).

Place a rack or tea towel in the bottom of a large pot (this prevents the jars from touching the bottom of the hot pot and breaking). Using canning tongs, place the jars in a large pot, and fill it with enough hot water to cover the jars. Slowly bring to a boil and boil for 10 minutes. Using the canning tongs again, transfer the jars to a cooling rack and let them sit undisturbed for 24 hours. The preserve should be stored unopened in a cool dry place, and will last for 6 to 12 months. Once open, store in the fridge for up to 2 months.

COOK'S NOTE: *Peaches, when perfectly ripe, are one of the greatest fruits of all time. As my friend Bobby says, "If the juice ain't running down your arm while you're eating it, you ain't got a good one!"*

Bobby Lax

TOFINO, BC

Most people in Tofino know Bobby Lax as the man behind the Tofino-Ucluelet Culinary Guild and the host of the Friday Funky Food Hour on the community radio station. To me, though, he's more like a son. Bobby started working with me in the SoBo truck when he was just 22. He had heart and passion and was like a sponge, absorbing everything I could teach him. He started early and stayed late, always offered to help with the young ones and developed a great rapport with my mother. That says a lot about a 22-year-old man. He's committed his life to making great food available to people on the coast, but he wasn't always the professional food lover that he is now. "I used to take peanut butter and jam to school every day," he remembers. "When I was young, it was all I wanted to eat. I didn't realize how significant a role food would play in my life

until later on. A friend and I started a meal delivery service in university—we spent one Saturday cooking for 15 hours straight, and it didn't even feel like work. Since then, I haven't thought of doing anything that didn't have to do with good food."

Through the Culinary Guild, he's carved out a unique niche in our community by connecting local chefs to fabulous but affordable ingredients that support the region's food system. "Independent food producers are some of the most honest, efficient and caring individuals we have in society," he says. "Their unwavering sense of integrity to the food they provide for others pushes me to be better at my job and as a human being. I never need a contract, just a handshake. That's always been enough."

Acknowledgements

Thank you:

To my mom, for being my biggest fan and supporting us in our venture. Without you, there would be no SoBo. Your love and faith in me has seen me through a lot of hard times. To my dad, who always believed I would be a chef even when I could not see it.

To Barkley and Ella, for being patient with me every time I said, "Kids, just give me a few more minutes and I promise I will be done" while I worked on this project.

To Jeremy Koreski for taking a risk with food photography when you could have been in the surf. Your images are so true to the heart and soul of SoBo. And thank you for teaching me about natural light and forcing me to think outside of the box.

To Lindsay Paterson of Appetite by Random House, for holding my hand every step of the way and steering me through this uncharted territory.

To Robert McCullough, who saw the first version of the SoBo cookbook almost a decade ago and encouraged us to make it a reality.

To Andrew Morrison, for your wordsmithing and for nudging me into the arms of Random House.

To Michelle Sproule, for being the voice of reason. And thank you for your patience, for finding all my lost files, for putting all my ducks in a row, and for loving my family like you do.

To Sarah Davies Long, for bringing style and beauty to SoBo and to this book. Every moment our families spent together on this project was special and we will cherish those memories.

To Malcolm Johnson, for being with us from the beginning of this project and still being there, my clean up hitter, at the finish. You saved me.

To Sarah McLachlan, one of the most talented and inspirational women in the world. Thank you for being a SoBo fan and for taking the time to say so in this book.

To Baku of ThinkTank Design Inc., for guiding us in the right direction.

To the entire Lawson family, for opening up your home on Wickaninnish Island, where much of the shots were taken; for hauling all the food over by boat and walking it through the forest; for foraging for us and for loving us like your own. You are amazing and generous.

To George and Rosalie Swartz of the Post Hotel, for sharing your wealth of knowledge about hospitality, not to mention your workplace and your home. Your generosity never ends.

To Sharon and Chris of Sea Wench Naturals. How on earth could I live without you two?

To Orangutang Design, for hosting us at the farm. What a slice of heaven.

To our sous chef Jennie Bacinski, for being one of the hardest working players around.

To all the suppliers, foragers, farmers and fishers. Without you we are nothing. Seriously, it all starts with the ingredients. I honor you.

To all those who ground it out for us, been burned, cut, endured sore feet and aching bones but finished service, then scrubbed and cleaned on our behalf. We thank you.

To the townspeople of Tofino and Ucluelet, for supporting us and for keeping an eye on our kids while we are working. It takes a village.

A special thank you to pastry chef Jen Scott. You have worked with us for nearly a decade and had my back every step of the way.

Suppliers

SoBo owes everything to the wonderful group of suppliers who bring us fresh, tasty ingredients every day, so we'd like to introduce to you some of our key suppliers. Check out their websites, give them a call or stop by the next time you're in the area.

Alderlea Vineyards
1751 Stamps Road
Duncan, BC, V9L 5W2
www.alderlea.com
250-746-7122

Avalon Farm (see page 43)
8286 Faber Road
Port Alberni, BC, V9Y 9B4
www.avalonfarm.ca
avalonfarm@shaw.ca
250-724-6821

**Basil Olive Oil Products Ltd
(see pages 26 and 33)**
Pitt Meadows, BC, V3Y 1W3
www.basiloliveoil.com
sales@basiloliveoil.com
604-460-0087

Blue Mountain Vineyard and Cellars
2385 Allendale Road
Okanagan Falls, BC, V0H 1R2
www.bluemountainwinery.com
250-497-8244

Canadian Hazelnuts
6682 #7 Highway
Agassiz, BC, V0M 1A1
canadianhazelnut@telus.net
604-796-2136

Creekmore's Coffee
PO Box 555
Qualicum Beach, BC, V9K 1T1
www.creekmorecoffee.com
coffeecreek@shaw.ca

Freedom Farm
2099 Coleman Road
Courtenay, BC, V9J 1V8
www.facebook.com/freedom.farm.9
woroniak@telus.net
250-898-8413

GFS (Gordon Food Service)
1700 Cliveden Avenue
Delta, BC, V3M 6T2
www.gfscanada.com
info@gfscanada.com
1-800-663-1695

Green Lady Greens
1320 Pacific Rim Highway
Tofino, BC, V0R 2Z0
www.facebook.com/pages/Green
-Lady-Greens/525757174138174
greenladygreenstofino@gmail.com
250-725-3145

Horizon
5589 Trapp Avenue
Burnaby, BC, V3N 0B2
www.horizondistributors.com
generalinquiries@
horizondistributors.com
1-800-663-1838

Hoyne Brewing Co.
101-2740 Bridge Street
Victoria, BC, V8T 5C5
www.hoynebrewing.ca
info@hoynebrewing.ca
250-590-5758

Island Farmhouse Poultry
1615 Koksilah Road
Cowichan Bay, BC, V0R 1N1
www.farmhousepoultry.ca
inquiry@farmhousepoultry.ca
250-746-6163

JoieFarm
2825 Naramata Road
Site 5 Camp 4
Naramata, BC, V0H 1N0
www.joiefarm.com
info@joiefarm.com
1-866-422-5643

Katie Farm U-Pick
Mount Sicker Road
Westholme, BC, V0R 3C0
www.katiefarm.com
ifiwasarichfarmer@hotmail.com
250-710-2889

La Frenz Winery
1525 Randolph Road
Penticton, BC, V2A 8T5
www.lafrenzwinery.com
info@lafrenzwinery.com
250-492-6690

Lekkar Food Distributors Ltd.
2670 Wilfert Road
Victoria, BC, V9B 5Z3
www.lekkerfoods.com
1-877-788-0377

Lina's Garden
2281 Agar Road
Cawston, BC, V0X 1CZ
250-499-5492

Little Qualicum Cheeseworks
403 Lowrys Road
Parksville, BC, V9P 2B5
www.cheeseworks.ca
info@cheeseworks.ca
250-954-3931

Manitoba Harvest
69 Eagle Drive
Winnipeg, MB, R0C 3A0
www.manitobaharvest.com
1-800-665-4367

Naesgaard's Farm & Market
5681 River Road
Port Alberni, BC, V9Y 7G8
www.naesgaards.com
info@naesgaards.com
250-723-3622

Nanoose Edibles Organic Farm
(see page 96)
1960a Stewart Road
Nanoose Bay, BC, V9P 9E7
www.facebook.com/pages/Nanoose
-Edibles-Organic-Farm-BC
-Certified-Organic
neorg@telus.net
250-468-2332

Natural Gift Seafoods
1985 Stewart Road
Nanoose Bay, BC, V9P 9E7
www.naturalgiftseafoods.com
bryceid@telus.net
250-468-5241

Natural Pastures Cheese Company
635 McPhee Avenue
Courtenay, BC, V9N 2Z7
www.naturalpastures.com
cheese@naturalpastures.com
1-866-244-4422

OK Fruit
682 Rupert Road
Qualicum Beach, BC, V9K 1N2
www.okanaganfruit.ca
okfruit@gmail.com
250-951-3980

Out Landish Shellfish Guild
(see page 124)
Box 497
Heriot Bay, BC, V0P 1H0
www.outlandish-shellfish.com
outlandishshellfish@gmail.com
250-203-5108

Ponderosa Mushrooms &
Specialty Foods
1592 Kebet Way
Port Coquitlam, BC, V3C 5M5
www.ponderosa-mushrooms.com
info@ponderosa-mushrooms.com
604-945-9700

Sea Wench Naturals Ltd.
PO Box 78
Tofino, BC, V0R 2Z0
www.seawenchnaturals.ca
sales@seawemchnaturals.com

Soya Nova Tofu Shop
1200 Beddis Road
Salt Spring Island BC, V8K 2E5
www.soyanova.com
soyanova@shaw.ca
250-537-9651

Sysco Foods
2881 Amy Road
Victoria, BC, V9B 0B2
www.syscovictoria.com
reception@vic.Sysco.com
1-800-363-3331

The Fish Store
368 Main Street
Tofino, BC, V0R 2Z0
westpacificseafoods@seaviewcable.net
250-725-2264

Tofino Brewing Co.
681 Industrial Road
Tofino, BC, V0R 2Z0
www.tofinobrewingco.com
info@tofinobrewingco.com
250-725-2899

Tofino Coffee Co.
700 Industrial Way
Tofino, BC, V0R 2Z0
www.tofinocoffeeco.com
250-726-6016

Tofino Tea Bar
346 Campbell Street
Tofino, BC, V0R 2Z0
www.tofinoteabar.com
info@tofinoteabar.com
250-725-8833

Tofino Ucluelet Culinary Guild
(see page 259)
www.tucg.ca
info@tucg.ca
250-266-6665

Two Rivers Specialty Meats
180 Donaghy Avenue
North Vancouver, BC, V7P 2L5
www.tworiversmeats.com
info@tworiversmeats.com
604-990-5288

Yamato Trading Co. Ltd.
1050 Parker Street
Vancouver, BC, V6A 4B9
604-253-5022

Index

Photo Key

ii–iii Misty forest in the Megin River
valley

viii–ix Looking north across Cox Bay,
towards Tofino

x Old growth forest, north of Tofino

xii–xiii The original purple food truck,
Tofino Botanical Gardens, 2006

xiv View from Whaler Island, looking
north

4–5 View from the top of Lone Cone
mountain on Meares Island, looking
south over Tofino and the surrounding
islands of Clayoquot Sound

8 Browning Passage, with Meares
Island in the background

12–13 North Chesterman beach
at low tide, looking south towards
Frank Island

14 Bald eagle flying through the
Tofino harbor

16 Peter Devries, Canada's National
Surf Champion, at a surf break,
north of Tofino

50–51 View at the bottom of First
Street, Tofino, looking northwest at
sunset

114–115 View over Vargas Island at
sunset

172–173 Unnamed beach, north of
Tofino

232–233 Storm watching from
Chesterman beach, looking
southwest towards Lennard Island
Lighthouse

262–263 School of pilchards near
Tofino harbor, with the reflection of
an island in the water